R E A D Y !

A Step-by-Step Guide for Training the Search and Rescue Dog

By Susan Bulanda

Doral Publishing
Portland, Oregon
1994

Published by Doral Publishing.
10451 Palmeras Dr. Suite 225 West, Sun City AZ 85373-2001
Printed in the United States of America.
Copyedited by Luana Luther.
Cover design by Fred Christensen.
Drawings by Marcus Adkins, Nina Bondarenko and Joseph T. McNichol.

Third Printing, 2000

Library of Congress Number: 93-74002
ISBN: 0-944875-41-6

Bulanda, Susan.
    Ready:A Step-by-Step Guide for Training the Search and
Rescue Dog/ Susan Bulanda. –Wilsonville, OR : Doral Pub.,
c1994.

170 p. : ; 28 cm.

Includes index.
ISBN: 0-944875-41-6

1. Search dogs–Training. 2. Rescue dogs–Training.
I. Title.

SF428.55.B   636.7'0886 dc20

Acknowledgements

Because a book such as READY! is a detailed and exacting task, it is impossible to do it entirely alone. First and foremost, I owe a debt of gratitude to my husband Larry who has been a SAR dog handler just a little bit longer than I have. He has probably sacrificed the most by losing me for endless hours to my computer. Next, I want to thank Bill Dotson who was the first person to suggest that I write this book. To have someone as well-respected as Bill believe in me was a tremendous encouragement. I am deeply grateful to Professor Ron Eltzeroth who spent hours doing the first critique of my manuscript. I also want to give a hearty thanks to Cathy Bales, Judy LaBelle, and Caroline Hebard for reviewing my manuscript in its early stages. I want to offer a special "thanks" to Ken Boyles for his confidence in me. His concept of working with contaminated scent articles was a genuine inspiration. I want to thank the many SAR people who continued to support me as I worked on the manuscript—especially the members of my unit who have been patiently waiting for a copy of this book.

Dedication

To my father,
whose gentleness, honesty and love of mankind
has been a lifelong inspiration to me.
And to my mother,
whose love of animals has been a lifelong example.
I also want to dedicate this book to all of the rescue people
who sacrifice their time and risk their lives
so that others may live,
especially the behind-the-scenes, quiet support people
who make the search a success.
They have the inglorious jobs
that never make the headlines
or receive recognition.

CONTENTS

Introduction

Why write a basic, step-by-step guide for training a search and rescue (SAR) dog? Because, as the use of dogs for search and rescue work becomes more prevalent, there is an increased need for people who are experienced SAR dog trainers. Unfortunately, these people are few. There are also few books available on the subject. It is difficult for interested people to learn how to train their dogs for search and rescue work unless they live near an SAR unit. This book does not cover the volumes of knowledge needed to use an SAR dog effectively; however, it covers the mechanics of how to train an SAR dog to do his job. Further, we caution that this book will not make the SAR dog-handler team operational; canine SAR work involves much more than just using the dog.

It is my intention to present information on a number of methods for training dogs for SAR work. However, the techniques are as varied as the number of trainers who use them. If you are already a member of an established canine SAR unit, you should follow the directions of your trainer and use the procedures already established. Some units recommend a different order to make a dog operational and may not require that training follow the exact outlines suggested at the end of this book.

There are a number of ways a dog can be trained. The dog can be an airscenting dog who does not look for a specific scent; a tracking dog who is scent-specific and closely follows the actual footfalls the person leaves; a trailing dog who will follow a specific scent in the area in which a person travelled; and the scent-specific, airscenting dog who will airscent a specific person.

Dogs are used for many kinds of search work: wilderness, water, collapsed building, disaster, cadaver, avalanche and evidence. In order to be search-ready, a dog must be able to perform the kind of work in which you wish to specialize. This can be one type or all types of canine search and rescue. Dog handlers must also be trained to SAR unit standards in the related search and rescue specialization. Most units require the handler to be trained in first aid, orienteering, communications, and survival. Depending upon where you plan to operate, you may need special training to handle the weather and terrain you may encounter, such as mountain climbing, rappeling, cave work, or whitewater rescue and safety. It is also a good idea to take a course in managing the search function (MSF or MSO). Even if you never function as an incident commander, it is helpful to know what is going on and how you can help.

Disaster work also requires extensive training beyond the standard SAR training. It is very important that the handler receive training in disaster first aid, and handling hazardous materials, as well as in the specific skills associated with disasters such as avalanches, mud slides, etc.

As much excellent information exists on training a dog for tracking/trailing, I do not go into detail on this subject, but offer an overview and suggestions on how to start training in tracking/trailing for SAR work.

Canine search and rescue is a very rewarding activity. I have been involved in SAR work since 1984, and I am hooked for life. While everyone has a reason for getting involved, I have found that the bond that develops between my dog and me when doing SAR work is much deeper and somehow different from any other I have experienced. I am working with a dog in a real job. Maybe it is because of the high levels of both "bad" and "good" stress connected with SAR work, but the dogs seem to know that there is a difference between SAR work and other work, and they respond intensely. I am amazed anew when I see a dog work out a problem and demonstrate an admirable ability to do SAR work. It is a real pleasure to work with a dog as a team and to watch a well-trained dog in action. SAR dogs do not work for you, but with you.

While I use "he" in this book to refer to all canines and all handlers, I want to make it clear that both male and female dogs and male and female humans can do the job well. As it is with humans, it is a matter of the individual dog's desire to do the work, not the breed or sex. I use "he" only for literary convenience.

—Susan Bulanda
Pottstown, Pennsylvania

September 1993

PART 1
GETTING STARTED

Chapter 1
HISTORY

The first documented cases of dogs used for search and rescue were the dogs at Mount St. Bernard Hospice, St. Gothard and other Alpine passes. There is no record of the first time a dog was employed for search and rescue, but by researching available documents, we can learn when the use of dogs for search work developed. A detailed record dated in 1698 does not indicate that the hospice monks were using dogs at that time; however, by 1800, use of dogs for search and rescue was well entrenched at the hospice.

A letter, published in the 1910 book, *War, Police, and Watch Dogs* by Major E. H. Richardson, written by the Father Superior of the Mount St. Bernard Hospice to the editor of the *Illustrated Kennel News*, reads:

Dear Sir,
The information which I can give you about our dogs is not very extensive.

As regards their origin, nothing certain is known. In 1698 they do not seem to have been used for the assistance of travelers, because a minute account written by a monk who lived at that time does not make any mention of them, although he carefully described when and how the monks and the Hospice servants went in search of travelers, to which parts of the pass they proceeded, and what was given to the victims when found to revive and comfort them; but this chronicler does not refer in any way to the dogs. And if dogs had been used at that epoch for rescue work, that omission would indeed be astonishing, as that same monk actually mentions the dogs kept at the Hospice to turn the roasting-spit in the kitchen.

In 1800, however, the use of the dogs for the work of mercy had become habitual. To that period belongs the famous Barry, whose intelligence was the means of saving so many lives, and whose image, preserved by the art of the taxidermist, is in the museum at Berne.

Barry was credited with saving many lives during his lifetime. He was killed by a traveler who, stranded in a snowstorm, mistook Barry for a wolf and stabbed him. Despite his wounds he returned to the Hospice to alert the monks of the lost person. By the time the monks rescued the man, Barry had died.

In 1817, there is another authentic record of a dog who, of his own accord, aroused the attention of the monks by his barking and restless running forward and back again. The monks followed him, and he led the way to a very desolate and abandoned hut, where they actually found a poor fellow who had sought shelter there from the snowstorm, and was already unconscious. Since then, the dogs have frequently saved lives. When the weary travelers lose themselves in the pathless snow wilds, the dogs follow their traces, and show them, so to say, to the monks or servants. But the ordinary and most important service which the dogs render us is to act as guides when, during the thick fogs,

Major Richardson and his Ambulance Bloodhound in the trenches at Melilla in the Spanish War, 1909.

An Airedale assisting a nurse.

the violent storms, or in the night, the uncertain paths are quite hidden by the snow. A well-trained dog hardly ever loses his way, and even when the snow lies fifty to eighty centimeters on the ground, he will follow exactly the direction of the narrow footpath, and, as they are called up here in the mountain, the piom. One of our most famous dogs, who was named Drapeau, and who died in 1899, would go sometimes quite alone on to the mountain to look for travelers. He used to stop for a time at the point where they were likely to pass, and then return leisurely to the Hospice . . .
Le Prieur De L'Hospice

By 1899 in Europe, military ambulance dogs were used to search for wounded soldiers as well as for missing persons during peace time. The British Army Corps had a military ambulance dog program supervised by General Von Blumenthal in 1899. Richardson gives a good idea of how successful the military ambulance dogs were: "The report on a trial by a Prussian Jaeger Regiment states: 'The performances of the ambulance dogs exceeded all expectations. Under the most unfavorable circumstances—a broiling sun, among total strangers, in close overgrown country unknown to the dogs, an entire lack of scent except that of numerous foxes and other game they carried out their work wonderfully.'"

French war dog bringing means of locating wounded soldier.

Later, the writer continues: "[Ambulance dogs] carry on their backs a small parcel, marked on the outside with a red cross, and containing a length of bandage and small flasks of brandy and of water. On finding a wounded man, the dog allows him, if he is able, to unfasten the packet and make use of its contents; if he can then manage to walk, the dog leads him to where the field hospital is at work, to give him proper medical dressing; if not, the dog trots off to fetch the searchers, whom it guides to the man it has found. The dogs are said to show great intelligence in their work, and may be compared to the famous dogs of St. Bernard."

It is interesting to note that the dogs worked in adverse conditions—the heat of the day. The dogs also had to make decisions based on each find. He either had to lead the wounded back to a field hospital, which moved around as the battle progressed, or get the searchers (who were also on the move) and bring them back to the wounded man.

While Major Richardson clearly stated that any dog can do the work, he seemed to prefer Border Collies, Airedales, Bloodhounds and German Shepherds. It is also interesting that, based on early photos of Major Richardson's Bloodhounds, they worked off leash. As for alert methods, there were three basic ways the dogs were taught to lead a searcher to the wounded man. One method was to return to the handler, and by shuttling back and forth, lead the handler to the wounded; another was to stay with the wounded and bark; and the last method was to put the dog on a long leash and follow. Major Richardson made clear that no one method is best, and what will work for one dog may not work for another.

Based on the work done by these early pioneers, people in the United States developed the Red Cross Dog, also known as the casualty dog, for use during the Second World War. These dogs performed in much the same manner as the ambulance dogs of Europe.

Today, much of the SAR dog training done in the United States is based on the methods used to train the military dogs. The dog's function was to aid the medical rescue personnel in finding wounded soldiers on the battlefield. The dog was taught to ignore walking, standing, or marching soldiers, and locate those who were lying down or sitting. The herding breeds and retrievers were preferred and no dog that was vicious, a continuous barker, or prone to fight with other dogs was used. It generally took three months of intense training to qualify a dog for the military program. In modern SAR training, the dog is taught to locate people in an upright and moving position as well as those who are on the ground or hiding. When the military dogs were trained, the victim always ignored the dog, whereas in SAR training the victim plays a more active role in the lessons. Except for this difference, the training programs for the military and SAR dog are very similar.

Two German Shepherd ambulance dogs, World War I.

Chapter 2
The Functions of the SAR Dog

In order to choose the right dog or to socialize and train a dog you already have, you must have a good idea what the SAR dog is expected to do. The details of each type of SAR work can vary widely as dictated by working conditions, but the dog's main job will remain the same.

TYPES OF SEARCH AND RESCUE DOGS

Most people associate the Bloodhound with tracking and trailing search work. However, it is only one of several breeds of dogs used for this work. Any dog with a good nose can be an effective tracking/trailing dog, and, in fact, there are many Bloodhounds who do not have the sense of smell good enough to be an effective SAR dog. Scenting ability in both the airscenting and trailing dog should be judged according to the individual dog's ability and not according to breed. The major restrictions a dog will face are his physical ability to do the work and his desire to work. While any breed is able to work, features such as a short nose (any of the pushed-in face dogs), long back (Dachshund), or short legs or short stature (Bulldog) will render a dog incapable of doing SAR work. The breeds most commonly used are hunting, herding, and working dogs. A dog bred to work the field will have the physical ability as well as the desire to do SAR work. To understand better what type of dog is best, consider the work the search dog must do.

Scout doing some wilderness airscenting.

Tracking Dog

The tracking dog keeps his nose in the actual footprints of the victim and follows them step by step. He pursues a specific scent identified by the handler from an uncontaminated scent article. Weather conditions dictate the amount of time after the victim is missing that the tracking dog can still work. In certain conditions, the scent may not last long. Typically, the tracking dog works on-leash. In most cases, it is preferred that no other searchers are in the tracking dog's search area.

Trailing Dog

The trailing dog does not work the track step-by-step, but works a few feet from the actual track. He needs a scent article and has the same limits regarding scent and weather as the tracking dog. The trailing dog may work either off-leash or on-leash. As with the tracking dog, the trailing dog works best with no one in his search area.

Airscenting Dog

The airscenting dog is trained to sense any human scent in the area; he does not need a scent article. He can work an area in which there are other searchers or where other searchers have passed through. He works with his head up or tracks/trails with his head down; in other words, the airscenting dog puts hisnose wherever the scent is. There are no time limits or weather restrictions as there are with the tracking/trailing dogs. The airscenting dog usually works off-leash in a grid pattern.

Dog and handler being lowered from helicopter. Drawing by Nina Bondarenko.

Scent Discriminatory Airscenting Dog

The scent discriminatory airscenting dog looks for a specific scent but works in the same manner as the airscenting dog. He performs off-leash. The dog works in the same manner as the non scent-specific airscenting dog but is scent specific.

TYPES OF SEARCHES

Wilderness or Large-Area Search

The wilderness search covers an area designated by the incident commander (IC or search boss) which can range in size from a fraction of an acre to hundreds of acres (one square mile equals 640 acres). The size of the search sector is usually determined by the terrain, the dog's ability, and the number of dogs available. The dog's job is to clear the area. It is up to the handlers to determine that the lost person is not in the area, as well as to find any evidence or clues related to the lost person. An airscenting dog's task is to indicate anything that has human scent, whether it belongs to the lost person or not. In a wilderness search, the dog/handler team will usually sweep in a grid pattern (with the dog off-leash) to find any human scent in the area or articles carrying human scent. The distance of the dog's sweep pattern is decided in part by the terrain being worked; however, the dog should be willing to range at least 50 yards away.

It is necessary for the dog to navigate whatever he encounters in the wilderness: crossing streams; swimming; going through or over obstacles such as hollow logs, culverts, or abandoned buildings; climbing over rubble or rock piles; and entering thick brush. For wilderness searches, the dog should give a readable alert (or indication) when he has found a person either dead or alive, or when he has found evidence.

Equally important, the dog should do a re-find—leading the handler directly back to the person or evidence. Some handlers train the dog to stay by evidence or cadaver (human body or body parts), and give a bark alert either sitting or lying down; whereas for the live victim, the dog returns to the handler and gives his alert. Some handlers prefer the dog give "passive" alerts for evidence and cadaver, and "active" alerts for live victims.

In whatever manner the dog works, under no circumstances should the dog touch or pick up the evidence. The position and location of the evidence are very important and can give the searcher or the police additional clues. In most cases, the police want to send the evidence to a crime lab—and dog saliva on the evidence is an additional source of contamination which restricts accurate analysis for identification.

A tracking/trailing dog can work on-leash, but should only alert when on the scent of the victim or the lost person.

When the dog/handler team has completed a sector of the wilderness, the handler should report his coverage, including the probability of detection (POD), scent clues, and articles found and their locations. The handler is expected to recommend whether the area needs to be re-searched or not. If a body is found, the handler should protect the area until the authorities arrive. If the person found is injured, the handler administers first aid to keep the individual comfortable and alive until qualified personnel arrive to transport him to medical facilities. A dog/handler team must work effectively for between eight to ten hours.

Evidence or Small-Area Search

Dogs are often called to look for evidence in a criminal case. Searches of this type usually involve a smaller area. The dog is required to search the area meticulously, working close to his handler with his nose to the ground. Some handlers like to use a different command for evidence searches so the dog knows he is looking for an object and not a person. Again, the dog is not allowed to touch the object. Airscenting dogs must be able to work off-leash, and tracking/trailing dogs work on-leash. Some handlers require that the dog

Labrador Retriever searching debris. Drawing by Nina Bondarenko.

Forest Service float plane and canoe with a Malinois Search and Rescue dog. Drawing by Nina Bondarenko.

continue to alert on the object until released to preserve the location of the article and related clues. The most practical method is for the dog to sit by the article and bark. This keeps the dog from running around the area and destroying additional evidence. The dog and handler must sustain a concentrated search of a small area for up to two hours.

Cadaver Search

Cadaver searching seeks a body or body parts. These may be buried or otherwise hidden from view, wrapped in material such as rags or carpeting, in the trunk of a car, hidden in plastic bags in trash bins, etc., or may be above ground, as in the case of an explosion or a plane crash. The dog works close to the handler and searches precisely. In the case of persons buried underground for a long time, the dog will alert on the scent in the soil rather than the scent of the body. Dogs have been known to find buried bodies decades old. Dogs are also used to find the charred remains of people who are burned in fires; they can also alert on human ash and bone fragments. It is important that the dog does not alert on an animal carcass.

The dog/handler team should be able to work from two to eight hours in 30- to 40-minute increments with a break long enough to refresh the dog. The length of the search and the working segments depend in

Doberman Pinscher searching in the wilderness. Drawing by Nina Bondarenko.

part on how meticulously the dogs are required to search. One search condition—known as a fine search—requires the dog to sniff every inch of ground. A fine search is exhausting for a dog and requires a slow, steady worker. Sometimes, the handler uses string lines to mark off the area to be searched and works the dog between the strings to be certain every inch is covered.

Water Search

Water searches involve using the dog to find the bodies of people who have drowned. The dog works from a boat as well as from the shore. Because of the current and the wind, it is often impossible for the dog to give an alert directly over the body; however, the dog must be able to follow the scent cone to the point where it exits the water surface. Sometimes, the dog enters the water and swims to the exit point, but usually he hangs over the side of the boat and gives an alert when he scents something. The dog should not alert on drowned animals. The various conditions under which the dog works determine how long he can sustain the search. If the dog is forced to breathe the fumes from the boat, his search time can be as short as 15 to 30 minutes. The dog is expected to be able to work 30 minutes to eight hours.

Avalanche Search

In an avalanche search, the dog works through the snow and gives an alert at the point where the scent comes out of the snow. The dog must start to dig immediately rather than perform a re-find; thus, digging is the alert in this situation. The dog can save a life by digging a tunnel to the victim, allowing him to get air. This is especially true for people who are trapped under the snow and near the surface. Avalanche searching can be either a hasty search or a fine search. A dog/handler team should be able to work an eight to ten hour shift with frequent breaks. However, if an avalanche victim is not rescued within 15 to 30 minutes after being buried, his chances of being found alive are slim. Most avalanche rescue is body recovery work.

Disaster Search

Disaster search refers to a wide variety of circumstances, covering all types of disasters, both man-made and natural, including but not limited to mud slides, rock slides, collapsed structures, earthquakes, tornados, explosions, and hurricanes. Any disaster can require a number of technical skills. There is no certainty that the victim is alive or dead and there can be multiple victims. The team may have to search burned-out buildings or areas that are buried in mud and/or debris. All accidents can be included in the disaster search: airplane crashes, boat accidents, auto accidents, train wrecks, etc. The dog must be able to handle all situations. Agility and control over the dog is required. The dog is required to work off- or on-leash, and to be directed to an area with the handler at a distance. The dog must work where there is heavy equipment operating nearby, people yelling and the general chaos of a disaster situation. The dog must not alert on clothes, furniture, animals, etc., but only on human bodies, dead or alive. It is also helpful if the dog gives either a dead-body alert or a live-body alert. While it is all right for the dog to dig in a mud slide or avalanche, some handlers do not want the dog to dig in rubble for bodies. The dog is expected to work eight- to ten-hour shifts in 20-minute increments with rests. The handler reports scent clues and recommends where to focus rescue continuing efforts.

Handler Heidi Yamaguchi and Shiro practicing High Angle training. They are with the Dogs East group.

Chapter 3
Choosing and Socializing the Dog

Choosing the Dog

The first step in SAR training is choosing the dog. If you already have a dog, the only way to find out if he will do the work is to try him. Some dogs will fool you; an unlikely prospect may become the best SAR dog, while another seemingly prime candidate can turn out to be unmotivated or unsuitable for SAR work.

While it is true you can train any dog to do anything given the correct method and motivation, I believe if a dog does not show a genuine interest in the work early in training, it is not to the advantage of the SAR community and your unit to persist. To do a good job in adverse situations, the dog must love the work. Although it seems that certain breeds of dogs do better in search work, it really depends upon the individual animal.

A strong play-prey drive is one of the first signs to look for in choosing a good SAR dog. Dogs who do not have strong drives usually are not suitable for SAR work. Also, a variety of dog bred to work independently of people rather than for or with people is not SAR dog material. SAR dogs and their handlers work together as a team and form a very strong bond.

Because most people love their dogs deeply and develop a special attachment with them, it is easy to believe that the dog will perform effectively and cheerfully, when in reality he may not be cut out for SAR work. It is important to remain objective about your dog. SAR work is demanding, and many dogsdo not work out. Ideally, an SAR unit will have a training evaluator. Also, it is a good idea to ask a trainer from another unit to evaluate your dog. Someone's life may depend upon you and your dog's skills.

Qualities

The ideal SAR dog is calm, bold and confident, not aggressive or overy dominant.

He is people-motivated and eager to please.

He prefers using his nose rather than making a visual find.

The dog is curious in new situations or about new objects.

He has the size and build to handle all types of obstacles in the city and the wilderness.

He is young and healthy enough to give years of service.

Consider that the average working dog will start to lose his stamina between eight and nine years of age. For some breeds, the prime working age ends between five and seven years old. When you consider that it can take up to 18 months to get a dog/handler team fully operational, clearly a younger dog with a longer working life is a more practical choice.

The ideal breeds to train for SAR fall into the working, herding, and sporting dog categories. However, there is no one breed that is better than another for SAR work. Americans tend to have a narrow view of which dogs are best for SAR work and forget there are many breeds that are successfully used for SAR work in other countries, such as the Border Collie, the Beauceron (a European-style Boxer), Giant and Medium Schnauzers and the Airedale. These breeds have not yet had a chance to prove themselves in the United States. Also, some of the best SAR dogs are mixed-breeds. One important consideration is that the dog not have any genetic defects. Dogs bred solely for conformation show purposes should be cautiously evaluated; they may not have the working ability required for the demands of SAR work.

Socialization

The first requirement of an SAR dog is that he is confident and social. Aggression toward people or

A SAR dog should feel comfortable with all types of aircraft.

animals is absolutely unacceptable. The dog must keep his head under high stress situations when his handler as well as the people around him are very excited. The dog must handle all types of noise and unusual physical conditions, such as rumbling, unstable ground and strong odors.

To ensure that a dog will meet the requirements of SAR work, you must socialize him. The younger a dog is, the more easily he will become socialized. The ideal age to start is six or seven weeks. Until the dog has had the necessary shots and is nine to ten weeks old, primary socialization should take place in the home. You will want to have adequate control over your dog, which will require some obedience work. Start puppy training at home a few days after you get your pup, or right away with an older dog. The training process is a form of socialization and helps to develop a bond between you and the dog.

Socializing your dog is not difficult but it is time consuming; it requires more than taking your dog with you wherever you go. Plan to introduce your dog to different situations. Depending upon where you live, socialization could involve an all-day outing. Take him out among people. The dog must get used to and accept strangers petting him. He must allow children to hug him around the neck and kiss him on the face. In a search situation, the dog is often the focus of hope and a form of reassurance to the victim, the victim's family and friends. It is common for people to hug the dog when a victim is found.

It is important to walk the dog in both city and country settings. Focus on the smells and sounds of the city, including noise generated by construction work, such as heavy equipment, jackhammers, etc. Heavy construction will also produce vibrations through the ground. The dog should smell different fuels—from a distance—given off by diesel equipment, gas, propane, and electrical equipment. This is especially important for handlers training for disaster work.

A properly socialized dog is essential for SAR work. Kuma, a Rottweiler and friend.

Coming down in Berlin, November 1991.

It is also a good idea to get the dog accustomed to different footing and flooring. The dog should be walked on different ground and floor surfaces, including slick, rough, uneven, and moving surfaces (such as elevators).

Expose the dog to the sights and smells of the country, including farm equipment. He must not be frightened by, nor want to chase, livestock and wild animals.

Introduce him to the wilderness. He should swim in lakes and ponds; cross streams; navigate logs, boulders, ravines, gullies, and hills. The dog should walk through and near various kinds vegetation. Introduce him to cliffs, and teach him to be wary of them. (This is especially important since a dog's sense of distance and depth perception are not as good as a human's.) The dog should experience the feel and sound of strong wind and weather in both country and city environments.

Part of his socialization should include trips to small and large airports. If possible, the dog should experience flying in small aircraft and helicopters. If flying is not possible, load him into and out of aircraft while the motor is both off and running. Also, introduce the dog to boats, both as observer and as a passenger.

Socialization also includes visiting nursing homes and being with people who move slowly or who use special equipment to get around. The sight of a person in a wheelchair or on crutches can upset a dog who has never seen this before.

Be inventive. Use your imagination and introduce your dog to every situation you can envision. You will still encounter conditions on a search that you have not anticipated. But if your dog has confidence and trust in you as well as in himself, he will handle whatever comes his way.

The most important aspect of socialization is to be sensible. Don't introduce your dog to situations in a way that frightens him; this defeats the purpose of socialization.

Initial shyness or insecurity in a puppy is not a matter of great concern. It shows that the pup needs more socialization. Many puppies go through a period of shyness that they overcome with proper handling. However, if the dog is a year old or more, shyness and fear warrant more concern. The older the dog, the more serious the problem. If the older dog does not adjust to strangers within a few training sessions, and with a concentrated socialization effort by the owner, the dog's suitability for SAR work should be seriously evaluated by the training director of the unit, a competent dog trainer, or a canine behaviorist.

One of the popular dog training philosophies teaches that the owner of the dog must assume the dominant "alpha" role with his dog. This method teaches that all interaction between dog and owner should be with owner dominance in mind. The alpha-dominant philosophy eliminates some interaction between dog and owner that usually takes place as play. For example, this system teaches that is not desirable to allow puppies to mouth people. Some trainers even claim it is not acceptable to allow the dog to stand over you, stare at you, or for you to hug the dog.

Rather than this complete owner dominance, it is important for a young puppy to be allowed to use his mouth to play with humans, as well as with other animals. First, teach the dog to develop bite inhibition, or learn to control his mouth. Second, teach him that biting is not acceptable. The potential SAR dog must learn to relate to people in a variety of situations. The dog who is forbidden to stand over a human, with the human in a prone position, may not know how to relate to such an experience in an SAR setting.

The dog must learn to play with his owner and with other people. All interactions with the dog are important parts of socialization. The dog should learn how to roll around with people, play excitedly, have people (especially children) crawl under him, over him, reach over him, touch him and so on. In other words, do what you want to do. Show affection by holding his head and gazing into his eyes while whispering sweet nothings. It is a key element of the dog/human bond.

Success comes in communicating to the dog the difference between play and work. The play sessions should be defined as play and work defined as work. If the dog is not sure when he is doing what, he will be confused. During training or work, the dog must be obedient, and play must be controlled. This teaches the dog to be contained when he is excited. It also builds the dog's trust and confidence in the handler. During play it is okay to let the dog win and play at being alpha with you, as long as the play ends with you in control. The best way to establish your alpha position is to run through the obedience commands quickly and give the dog hearty praise for obeying the commands. What most confuses the dog are mixed messages. For example, when the dog does something the owner does not want, the owner says "no" to the dog in a meek voice, and pats the dog, thinking the pat is a gentle slap. In reality, the dog understands the pat as praise for the behavior. Dogs do not understand English, and when the tone of voice is meek, the dog interprets the owner's reaction as praise for behavior the owner does not want.

Play interaction with your dog is important socialization. The dog should be encouraged to play with many different people of all sizes, races, sexes, and ages.

A well-socialized dog can handle all situations. Marcia Koenig's German Shepherd Orca in helicopter. Photo courtesy of Bob Koenig.

Chapter 4
Concepts of Dog Training

While it is not the purpose of this book to focus on the concepts of dog training, you cannot prepare a dog for SAR work without some understanding of how to train. Keep in mind, techniques vary as widely as the trainers who use them.

The Job at Hand

Before you can teach a dog to do a job, you must understand the job yourself. Be sure to review the details of the task and break it down into the smallest steps possible. Remember, at first the dog does not have the slightest notion what of you want. He just wants to please you.

Dogs do not Speak English

This is one of the most important concepts to keep in mind. Not only do dogs not speak English, but as far as we can tell, their communication system is not based primarily on sound. Therefore, it is reasonable to assume they do not even think in verbal terms. What is important to a dog is your body language, including your facial expressions and your tone of voice. Because our body language and tone of voice reflect our attitude, it is important to be positive while training a dog. If you do not believe your dog can do the work, you handicap the dog's ability to learn. The dog reads your negative attitude easily through body language.

Equipment

There are many different types of equipment available to use to train a dog. Generally speaking, use the following: As a permanent collar to be left on the dog at all times, (except for situations in which it is not safe to have any collar on your dog at all) try the *Premier* collar made by Premier Pet Products. This is a combination buckle and choke collar that will not harm your dog if properly fitted. The *Premier* leash and collar are suitable for training as well as search work. The *Premier* six-foot leash is good for training because it is flexible and can easily be packed away. These products are strong and hold up. You also could use a standard buckle collar.

Strictly for training purposes, the *Halti* head harness or the *Premier Easy Walker* is suitable. The head harness allows you to control the dog that is young or otherwise easily distracted by turning his head toward you so you can teach him to focus on you or pay attention. It is indispensable when teaching a dog to avoid something.

Do not use a chain choke collar because it can be too harsh. It can damage a dog's neck and spine. You should NEVER use a prong collar or shock collar to train a dog.

Proper Tone of Voice

Because dogs do not speak English, the tone of your voice is critical. With body language, tone makes up the primary means you use to communicate with your dog. You must make your tone of voice directional, and no-nonsense, rather than questioning, dictatorial, hysterical, and loud. A dog has an acute sense of hearing. A lack of response is not because the dog does not hear you; it is because he chooses not to listen to you. Do not yell at your dog. Speak in a soft-to-normal volume. When the dog does what you want, raise the tone of your voice, not the volume, to praise the dog. When you correct the dog, lower the tone to suit the correction. The most severe correction should be a growling sound.

Negative Reinforcement

Negative reinforcement is different from punishment. Negative reinforcement is not pleasant and is something that can be stopped by ending the unacceptable activity. Auto manufacturers use negative reinforcement, the annoying buzzer or bell, to get us to hook our seat belts and close our doors. When we hook the belt, the sound stops. After awhile, we hook the belt immediately to prevent the noise. Thus, the negative reinforcement trains us to do what the auto manufacturer wants. An example of the use of negative reinforcement with dogs is the *Invisible Fence* that gives the dog a bell warning if he comes close to the boundary, followed by an electric shock for crossing it. If the dog wants to eliminate the shock, he moves away from the fence line.

Punishment

Punishment techniques are different from negative reinforcement. Punishment is applied whether the activity stops or not. Punishment is a coercive act a handler inflicts on a dog as a reaction to unwanted behavior. The coercive act often causes some degree of pain or discomfort to the dog. Examples of punishment are a shock from a shock collar, a painful sound, slaps, punches, pinches, or leash jerks. Although punishment works, it is not conducive to the dog's well-being and desire to please. Punishment is usually the reaction of a frustrated dog owner. When you punish a dog because of frustration, you tend to overcorrect or over-punish. It is easy to give in to the desire to punish more severely when a lesser level of punishment doesn't produce immediate results. Some dogs who are overcorrected to the point of being defensive will bite.

Punishment can inhibit undesired behavior, but only if it is used properly by someone trained in correct techniques. As a rule, the SAR dog handler will find that avoiding both punishment and negative reinforcement will produce the best SAR dog. Instead of punishing your dog, show him what to do. Communicate to the dog that the behavior he has exhibited is not correct. To do this, lean forward, make eye contact; then in a deep growling voice, tell your dog "No." As soon as the dog stops the unwanted behavior, praise him. If you find you are correcting a dog more than you are praising the dog, it is time to reevaluate your training technique.

Teach and Show

When you train a dog, remember he does not have a clue what you want from him. You must structure your training to show the dog what to do and reward him for doing it. It is unfair to punish a dog for not doing what you want when he does not understand what is expected of him.

Commands

Whatever commands you decide to use, be sure to be consistent. A command should always result in an action, either on your part or the dog's part. He either obeys or you teach. Never stand and repeat a command to a dog. Remember, dogs do not speak English, so if you tell your dog to "Sit, sit, sit," he will not know that s-i-t is one word. He will think "Sitsitsit" is the command and will learn not to sit until the third command. By repeating commands, you also teach the dog that it is okay to respond when he feels like doing so, or that he does not have to respond at all. Rationalizing a dog's lack of response only encourages the repetition of the behavior because you allow the dog to disobey or obey in a way that is not acceptable to you. You must define the manner in which you want your dog to respond to a command and stick to it.

Be Inventive

Do not get into a rut of methods and styles. Different things work for different exercises. Not all methods work all of the time for all dogs. Do not hesitate to try different ways to communicate with and motivate your dog. Remember, dogs get bored, too.

Motivate

The key to successful dog training is to motivate your dog. A dog will never learn anything unless it is meaningful to him. Proper motivation makes the lesson meaningful. Use whatever works. If your dog works for food, use food; if he likes to play, use play as a reward. Many trainers use punishment to teach a dog. This method is especially undesirable for training the SAR dog. The dog must love the work and enjoy it. The dog who does SAR work because he is afraid of being punished will not work reliably, nor will he work as long.

Food Reward

Many traditional trainers absolutely refuse to use food as a reward. There is a continuing debate over this issue. When using food, be sure the focus of the reward is your verbal praise, petting, and then the food. To do this, give your dog a hearty "Good dog," then one or two quick pats on the head (no strokes), and then the tiny morsel of food. The whole process should only take 30 seconds. It does not matter what kind of food you use; however, it should be semi-moist, which will allow you to regulate the size of the tidbit. The reward should never be larger than a quarter-inch square. It is a tease, something the dog will work harder to acquire. The food must be desirable to the dog. It should not be given every time; intermittent reinforcement for the desired behavior is strongest. It should be gradually withdrawn and praise substituted. If you reward the dog for every correct act, the food will no longer motivate the dog.

Food training has some interesting points to consider. First, a dog who is fearful or in pain will not respond to a food reward. This means if you use a food reward successfully, your dog is learning in a non-fearful and non-painful environment. This atmosphere is necessary for the SAR dog. Some trainers claim the dog will work for food and not out of love for the owner. However, as long as your bond with the dog is strong, your dog will work for you out of love. The food is just a nice added motivation. You do not have to starve a dog to use a food reward because we are not talking about making the dog work to earn his meal, but merely to earn the special treat. If the dog does not perform to the level you want, you do not withhold his dinner. (Please note: due to the risk of torsion and bloat, it is not a good idea to work a dog right after he eats his dinner. Check with your veterinarian to learn more about torsion and bloat.) Food reward is a proven method commonly used in all levels of animal training. Earning the extra tidbit increases the dog's inventiveness in developing ways to earn his treat.

A study by Margaret Gibbs illustrates that dogs learn more quickly and are more eager to work when the reward is food. The study illustrates that food works much better than the traditional punishment techniques or hand signals.

Further support for the use of food as a reward comes from researchers at the Veterans Administration Medical Center in Sepulveda, California, who have discovered a dog's memory is enhanced by hormones released during feeding. The implication is that if a dog is fed after training, it will enhance his memory, enabling him to retain better what he has learned.

If food works, use it, but use it properly. Food is not meant to be a bribe for the dog, but a reward for proper behavior or performance. For two interesting articles on food reward, see *Pure Bred Dogs/American Kennel Club Gazette* (April 1990), "Food for Thought," by Patricia Gail Burnham and "To Treat or Not to Treat," by Margaret Gibbs.

Keep the Goal of Each Exercise in Mind

Often handlers get sidetracked while training a dog or they try to teach the dog too much at once. Be sure to identify the goal of the exercise and work toward it.

If Your Dog Doesn't Get It

If you find a dog doesn't get the idea, go back to the previous step and/or try different techniques or motivation methods. When your dog does not grasp what you are trying to teach him, it may be because you have not established the rules of obedience and/or the particular exercise. You may have given the dog the option of choosing whether he wants to work or not. Usually, he probably doesn't understand what you want him to do. Reevaluate the exercise and break it into smaller steps. For example, the dog will not stay for the long-down. To correct this, start by downing the dog and waiting for a few seconds before praising him. Increase the length of the down by increments of a few seconds until the dog understands he has to stay for the duration. As he stays for you, lengthen the down until you can walk around the corner of a building and the dog will stay. If you just walked away for 20 minutes without working up to it, the dog would never learn to stay.

If your dog has problems at any level of training, go back to the previous level and be sure he knows that before you advance to the next level. A dog should not move on to the next level until he can perform the previous level "in his sleep." This usually takes a week, working every day. When you first perform an exercise, the dog may seem to grasp it, but the exercise may not be fixed in his long term memory. Thus, by the next session, you may have to retrain the dog. This is especially true for immature dogs. Young dogs have not had experience and practice in learning how to understand you.

If Your Dog Refuses to Work

Sometimes you may believe your dog knows an exercise but is refusing to do it. Many people say this is stubbornness or defiance. It is really just a lack of response. There are several possible reasons for this behavior. He may not have learned the exercise thoroughly. All dogs learn at their own rate, and there is nothing you can do to change this. Another possibility is that the dog does not feel well—you must always check and rule out a physical reason for a lack of response. You cannot expect a dog who is in pain from an injury to work for you.

Also, you must take a close look at your training techniques. If you have slipped into the punishment mode of training, you may find that the more a dog is corrected as opposed to being praised or rewarded, the more his confidence and willingness to work diminish.

Often the handler gets angry if a dog refuses to work. Many people yell when they're angry. This, in turn, frightens a dog. Punishment causes more fear and results in less response. It becomes a vicious circle with few positive results.

You cannot teach when you are angry; you are reacting to the situation instead of being in control. To teach, you must be in control. If your dog makes a mistake, do not correct this by punishing him. Go back and prompt him to do the correct thing and reward him for doing it.

Occasionally, a dog may refuse to work or the quality of his performance may slip because you have become sloppy in your handling of the exercise. You may have inadvertently taught the dog to perform at a different level from what you intended. When you do not get the level of performance you want, reevaluate yourself as well as the dog.

You must also consider the possibility of burnout. If you suspect this, try giving him a few weeks off. Remember, SAR is very stressful, even to a dog. Also, if you are stressed or suffering burnout, the dog will react to your attitude.

There is always the problem of regression in training. For various reasons, the dog will seem to forget what he has learned. Often, this happens when training is discontinued for too long a time. The dog may be inadvertently untrained or retrained so that the former work is undone. In this situation, it is best to start over and retrain the dog. Usually, the retraining will take less time.

Short Lessons

Keep the lessons short. You will not bore or tire your dog, and he will like the work. Only after the dog has learned what to do can you work him for the longer periods necessary to qualify for SAR work. It is especially important to keep the lessons very short, 10 to 15 minutes, when you are training a young dog. The younger a dog is, the shorter his attention span. Five-minute lessons followed by five minutes of play, repeated three times for a total of 15 minutes, work well. You can work the dog for several 15-minute sessions throughout the day if the sessions are far enough apart that the dog does not become frustrated or bored. The training should always be fun for the dog. Practice of acquired skills can be more serious, but learning should be fun.

Age to Start

Dogs as young as eight weeks old can start with the games that lead up to search work. When deciding the age to start a pup, consider whether the pup is bonded enough to you, settled enough in his new home, and healthy. Allow about 10 to 12 weeks of age for this. When you start a very young puppy, keep the work light and give the dog time off. The SAR dog handler easily gets too intense too soon. This causes burnout in the dog and the handler.

Start Exercise Signal

You should have a signal to let the dog know that training or work is to begin and which type of work is expected. If you plan to cross-train your dog to do different types of work, the second point is very important. Your dog will know by your cue that he is to do search work as opposed to obedience, tracking, etc. Some people use a special collar or harness to signal the dog what type of work is expected of him. The signal could also be a particular short routine, but it should not be the actual command to begin. For example, you can let your dog know training time has arrived by repeating a particular phrase, such as "Let's go train," before you begin the training. Or, the signal can be a short routine such as slapping the dog's side and telling him to get ready for work. The main function of the start exercise signal is to build up the dog's excitement and anticipation. Often in search work, the sight and sound of you getting your gear together will do this, but do not depend on this as your signal. Whatever you decide to use, it must be consistent.

End of Exercise Signal

Similar to the start exercise signal, this signal lets the dog know he is through. It is a release command or routine. Some people just give the dog the command, "Finished," or "Okay," which lets the dog know he is free from the work. The start exercise and end exercise signals are most important to use during training sessions; it must be clear to the dog when the training sessions begin and end.

Game Play Reward

This is the most important aspect of SAR dog training. Besides pleasing you, the reward game is strong motivation for doing the work. After awhile, the reward will be finding the victim; however, to make this transfer, the dog must have a pleasant or fun motivation for the find.

Not all dogs are play motivated. Some individual dogs (and some breeds) are very serious. Some people believe all dogs can learn to play and that those who do not play are the result of an "all work and no play" attitude by the owner. Still others believe animals do not play for fun, but that play is directed by instincts, which makes it a drive. For example, a Retriever has a drive to fetch objects, and is often called a compulsive retriever. Another example is the Border Collie's drive to gather livestock and herd them to the handler. Although both breeds have a different purpose for their behavior, the results are the same.

In training, a dog will be most satisfied if the game involves an activity that allows him to do what he was bred to do. The problem is that many breeds no longer have the drive to do what they were developed to do, and some breeds were formed to do things that do not lend themselves to the training games that simulate SAR work.

Nevertheless, you can teach your dog to play, or to have a meaningful routine with you that the dog will enjoy and anticipate. All that is necessary is a dog who likes to do things with you. Thus, the motivation in the routine is the dog's desire to interact with you; success depends on how strongly the dog is bonded to you.

When inventing a game for your dog, observe what he likes to do best and, providing it is acceptable behavior, incorporate it into a game. If you are training a hunting dog, you may find letting the dog search through your pockets for a tidbit may do the trick. Being inventive is the key. But, be sure to develop the game before doing search work. An SAR training session is not the time or the place to teach a dog his reward game. He has enough to learn as it is.

Be Consistent

If you keep changing techniques with your dog he will never know what you want. When you train your dog, be consistent in your method of praise, corrective tone of voice, corrective technique, and in the method you use to show the dog what you want. Also, use the same commands for the behavior you want. Don't do the recall with "Come" one time and "Come over here" the next time and expect your dog to understand.

Senses

Most owners are aware that a dog has a keen sense of smell and hearing, but there are misconceptions about the other senses. Vision is one sense that we are not be completely certain about. New research suggests dogs may not be totally color blind as previously thought. They do have a wider field of vision than humans. The size of the field of vision depends upon the shape of the skull and placement of the eyes. A dog can see for about 250 degrees, compared to 180 degrees for humans. The dog's binocular vision—the area he sees with both eyes—is much less than a human's; the dog's range is about 100 degrees, compared to a human's 140 degrees.

Some people contend that dogs have poor depth perception and distance judgment. This is an important fact to consider when teaching a dog SAR work. Poor depth perception and distance judgment can cause a dog to hesitate or to be reluctant to do certain exercises that involve jumping into or over objects, or from one object to another. These exercises must focus on building the dog's confidence and judgment.

Dogs do see much better at night than humans, which helps during night searches and searching in dark, enclosed areas. While dogs do not see as well as humans, they do detect movement much better than humans. There is no research to suggest that herding and sighthound breeds have better vision than other breeds of dogs; it is anyone's guess whether they see better or are just more visually tuned in.

Another sense that people are often not aware of is the dog's sense of touch. Dogs have touch pads on their skin that are sensitive to pressure. A dog's hair is connected to sensory nerves that allow the dog to feel when his hair moves. This is one way a dog can feel his way around small places such as caves and tunnels. This sense of touch also explains why dogs enjoy being petted as a reward for performing a command. But despite this sensitivity, dogs are not as aware of temperature differences as humans are.

One Handler

One person should handle and train the dog. Each person is different and handles the dog differently. While a dog is learning, multiple handlers can confuse the dog. Once the dog knows what he has to do, he can deal with different handlers. However, for SAR work, the dog and the handler are a team and work best when they work together. In the event two people want to handle the same dog, all work should be duplicated to develop a dual handler/dog team. Often a dog will do his job no matter who is behind him, but the handler may not feel confident working with the dog because he does not know how to read the dog.

Physical Warm-up

Although not a training technique, a physical warm-up is important. If the dog finds the exercises physically uncomfortable, he will be less willing to do the work. If he is injured during training, he will be even less willing to go back into the same situation. Therefore, to prevent injury and discomfort, it is important to give the dog a chance to warm up before doing any work that requires any exercise beyond walking. It is a good idea to let the dog run on a flat, easy surface, fetching a ball or other object as a warm-up. This provides an outlet for energy built up from anticipation during the car ride to the training area. It also allows the dog time to relieve himself. The length of the warm-up depends upon the weather and the age and energy level of the dog. Be careful the warm-up exercise does not tire the dog out.

Who Rewards the Dog

In an SAR exercise, one method used is for the handler and victim to both reward the dog, with most of the reward coming from the handler. At some stages of training, only the handler rewards the dog, while at other stages, both the victim and handler reward the dog. Some handlers think the method in which only the handler rewards the dog can cause problems. If the handler alone rewards the dog, the dog will have difficulty learning the re-find, and will not "find" the same victim twice. This is especially true for the submissive dog or puppy. At first (for the beginning problems), the handler runs in with the dog and praises the dog while it is with the victim. As the problem advances, the handler cannot keep up with the dog and praises the dog as he returns to the handler, thus rewarding the dog for the return, not the find or re-find. The dog thinks the exercise is finished and becomes confused if the handler asks the dog to find or re-find.

Have only the victim reward the dog to handle this problem. Trainers believe the dog will try hard to get his handler to the victim so the dog can get his reward. This method requires a dog who is strongly bonded to his handler. It also requires the handler to teach the dog to expect a reward from the victim.

By developing a training plan in which the victim rewards the dog, you motivate the dog to find the victim. This also rewards the dog for going right up to the victim and not hanging back. When the motivation is strong enough, the dog is drawn to the victim and an automatic re-find results.

However, sometimes the dog does not want to leave the victim because his desire for the reward is stronger than his desire to return to the handler. This problem can be worked out with training.

If you wish to use the victim-reward system for training instead of the handler/victim-reward system, just teach the dog the reward game, which can be a retrieve, tug-of-war, physical play with the dog, or a food reward (remember, be inventive and find something your dog likes). Then, have the victim initiate the reward at the point in the exercise when the handler would be rewarding the dog. In the re-find, some dogs can be rewarded each time they find the victim, on the find and re-find, or some may need to receive the reward only when the handler is next to the victim. If the dog is rewarded each time he contacts the victim, he is doing the find over and over.

Chapter 5
Getting Started

Pretraining

The first level of SAR training is often done with very young puppies. A handler can play some games with the pup prior to search training to prepare him for SAR work. Inside the house, have the pup search for objects, such as his toys. Sit on the floor with him and tease him with his toy. As he gets excited about grabbing the toy, hide it around the other side of your body or under your body, making the dog find it. Be sure to let the pup have the toy when he finds it. As he gets the hang of the game, hide the toy under furniture or in other places.

If you move this game outside, be sure the dog is secure in your yard or play area. Puppies often become distracted and can run into a nearby road. It is okay to do the outdoor exercises on a long leash. When you and the dog are out walking in the woods, often the dog will wander ahead of you. If the dog gets out of sight, call him and then duck behind a tree or some brush, making the dog search for you when he returns. A well-bonded pup will come back and look for you. Be sure the pup can find you right away and be sure to praise him for coming to you. There are two benefits to this exercise. The dog learns to look for you and is rewarded for finding you, and it teaches the pup not to wander too far ahead of you.

The pretraining games can also be played with an older dog. Do not make the activity a formal lesson. Allow the dog to solve the puzzle or game in whatever manner he wants. These games will give you clues about your dog's natural abilities. Be observant. Learn from your dog. Look for specific mannerisms. When playing games with the dog, allow him to airscent or track, as he chooses.

Prior to and during SAR training, you must condition your dog to the situations encountered in SAR work. Conditioning can be fun during walks in the woods. Be sure your dog takes in a variety of sights and sounds. While exposing your dog to the obstacles he will encounter in SAR work, do not encourage a pup to do a great deal of climbing or jumping that will stress his joints. It is also not a good idea to allow a very young puppy to slip on slick surfaces. This stresses the pup's hips. (However, this does not mean the pup cannot be exposed to slick, flat surfaces. Use common sense when teaching young dogs to climb, go through tunnels, jump, and do all the things necessary for SAR work.)

Obedience

Obedience work in pretraining should be separate from SAR work. Obedience is important in maintaining control over your dog for off-leash field work. You will need off-leash control over your dog by the time you reach Level 3—a few weeks with most dogs.

The obedience training does not have to be competition training as done for obedience trials. Noncompetitive obedience is practical obedience that demands control over the dog, but does not require the dog to sit straight and do all the frills of competition obedience.

If you do plan to compete in obedience trials, remember not to pattern-train your dog. Pattern-training occurs when you always ask the dog to perform the same way. Most often, the handler does not vary the routine in which the dog works. The dog then learns to perform under specific circumstances in a certain way, without thinking. Remember the old milk horse who knew his route and did not need to be driven? Pattern-training hinders the dog's ability to handle SAR situations by inhibiting his ability to think for himself and work out the problems he faces.

Many SAR people talk about a dog's ability to perform what is called "intelligent disobedience." For example, a dog may insist you follow his lead to a victim even when you call him off because you decide the victim could not possibly be where the dog indicates. This situation presents a conflict for the dog. He has been trained to come when he is called, and he has been trained to lead you to a victim. The dog must decide which training he will obey. Some dogs will come back to you and give you the alert over and over until you understand. Others will refuse to come back and will try to get you to follow. You can teach a dog how to decide which command to obey by making the act of finding the victim the focus of the dog's training, emphasizing this through praise and reward. In other words, the dog's motivation to find the victim and get you next to the victim must be stronger than his desire to comply with his obedience command. You do not want an obedient dog who will come to you and leave the victim behind. This is a very important aspect of training, since everyone at one time or another does not believe his dog, or misses an alert.

One way to encourage and condition the dog's ability to think is to vary your training, in obedience as well as SAR. When taking your dog for a walk, do not make him heel all of the time. Allow him the freedom of

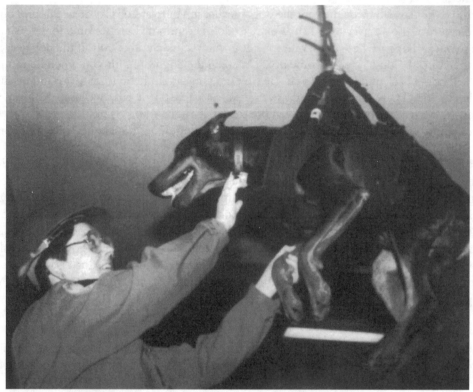

M. Limoger and Ira during lowering drills. Photo courtesy of SARDA.

the leash—without pulling. You can teach this to your dog by giving him a Don't Pull command when he gets to the end of the leash. By correcting him every time he pulls and praising him for not pulling, your dog will learn he can walk as far as the leash allows, but he cannot pull.

Give your dog every opportunity to experience as many different situations as possible. By working through experiences together, you will build team effectiveness with your dog. It will give your dog a wider base from which to draw in new situations.

Every dog trainer and owner, including SAR dog handlers, must at some point make a decision about a controversial, philosophical issue: Do dogs think? Your beliefs will dictate how you handle and train your dog, and will also influence your response to what your dog tells you. There are dog trainers and behaviorists who believe animals do not think. However, there is also a growing body of evidence that has convinced some scientists that all animals think more than we give them credit for. It is interesting that the debate is by no means a new one. A 1948 book, *Companion Dog Training*, Hans Tossutti of the New England Training School for Dogs, says:

> For years, controversy has raged regarding the dog's ability to reason . . . I agree with those scientists and intelligent students who claim that he cannot. I do not believe there is any such thing as reasoning power in dogs.

Of course the issue will never be resolved since no human can ever know for sure what goes on in the mind of a dog. After all, we don't even know for sure what goes on in the minds of other humans!

A Rottweiler puppy learning to go through tunnel. Drawing by Nina Bondarenko.

Gearing up for the real thing—a water search in Calgary, Alberta, Canada. Photo courtesy of SARDAA.

Cross-Training a Dog

"Cross-training" trains a dog to do more than one type of search work. One example is a dog who has been trained to airscent as well as to track. Some handlers and some units say you cannot successfully train a dog to do more than one type of search work; others have successfully cross-trained their dogs. It depends upon the handler as well as the dog.

If you would like to cross-train your dog, it is best to start with wilderness, airscenting work first (although some handlers feel very strongly that it is best to start with tracking first). Research the reasons for both opinions and figure out what is best for your dog.

Whether you train your dog to track or airscent first, wilderness training is the foundation for all other SAR dog training. It teaches the dog the concept that he must find a human. If you wish to teach your dog to track—and not to airscent at all—then start with that level of training.

One of the secrets of cross-training is to give the dog a clear message as to what you expect him to do. Your commands, as well as the props you use, must be unique for each type of work. For example, train off-leash for airscenting work and on-leash in a harness for tracking. This makes it clear which technique the dog is supposed to employ. These clues and signals are especially important for the dog who is just learning.

Keep a Record

Before you start any formal search training, prepare a log book. Every training session, whether it is with a unit or on your own in-between unit sessions, must be recorded. There are a number of reasons for this. If you are ever questioned in a court of law concerning your dog's qualifications, you will need a log book to prove your training methods, time spent, etc. Another reason is to keep a record of all the conditions in which you trained. This information gives you insight about how your dog works and why. Your log also provides a progress report on how your dog is doing, as well as the big picture. Sometimes by reviewing your procedures, you can determine how to solve problems. Never trust your work to memory.

Your log should detail your failures and your successes. (And, when you have a failure, be sure to write down what you plan to do to correct it.) The information in your log book should include:

1. The name of the dog.
2. The name of the handler.
3. Date.

4. Weather conditions: wind strength and direction, temperature, humidity, overcast, sunny, etc.
5. The location of the training.
6. Terrain features.
7. Any unusual events or conditions: unexpected people, sudden storms, wild animal activity, etc.
8. The problem as set up, executed, and the results.
9. The way the dog worked.
10. How you felt about the training and how you worked.
11. How long you spent on a problem.
12. Comments from the observer and/or victim.

Chapter 6
Wind, Scent and Dog

The Nature of Scent

We cannot smell what a dog smells, but we can help a dog find an available scent. To do this you must know about wind, weather, and terrain. These three elements affect how much scent is available and where the scent travels. Your understanding about the scent available to your dog will also determine how your dog performs. If you do not believe a dog can detect the human scent on a track that is more than three hours old, you will not train for an older track or give your dog a chance to prove his ability. If you do not think a dog follows human scent at all, you will not train the dog to be scent discriminatory in the same manner as someone who does believe a dog follows human scent. Some people believe a dog follows the crushed vegetation; others feel the dog follows the dead skin cells that fall off people as they walk. Still others think the dog picks up on a combination of both human scent and vegetation. We don't know exactly what a dog does or does not detect when following scent. What we can determine is how the scent behaves.

When SAR people talk about scent, they often speak of the scent cone given off by the victim. Scent-cone theory explains that the victim is the source of the scent, or the tip of the cone. As the scent leaves the victim, it fans out to form the base of the cone, becoming wider as it travels further away from the victim. It is the job of the search dog to seek the cone and follow it to its source.

In many respects, scent behaves in the same manner as liquids and smoke. Scent flows down a slope following the path of least resistance, such as a gully or drainage. It rises from its source, reaches a high spot in the air, loops back down to the ground, and collects in that spot. Scent can circle a number of times, leaving many pools of scent with no obvious line to the victim. The dog comes along, hits the spot, and cannot follow the scent to its source. Sometimes, if the origin of the scent is in a depression, such as a small valley, the scent can travel up the nearby slopes in much the same manner as smoke goes up a chimney. This is usually caused by the rise of warm air during the day, which carries the scent with it. The reverse can happen as the air cools and falls to the low areas, carrying the scent down with it, and trapping the scent in a drainage, or carrying the scent from a higher level down a slope to a low area. When this happens, the scent pools in the low area.

Terrain features such as tree lines, rock walls, and plowed fields can cause the scent to eddy, swirling around the trees, behind the wall, and traveling over the wall, leaking scent into a clearing. On dry, hot days with no noticeable breeze, the scent may rise straight up and the dog will not find the victim unless he walks over him. In rough terrain and in gusty, shifting winds, the scent can travel in many directions, collecting in nooks and crannies in the same manner as debris washed down a river. Scent clings to objects such as walls, brush, or low areas. If a victim is hidden in dense vegetation (especially vegetation with low broad leaves), it is possible for the scent to become trapped with little or no leakage.

Humidity increases the availability of scent for a dog, and scent that has "dried out" during the day may "revive" in the damp of the evening and morning or after a light rain. The dampness releases what has soaked into the ground. However, a downpour will wash the scent away.

Early morning, evening, and night are the best times for the dog to pick up scent. During the day is the poorest time for the dog to work. In the morning, as the ground warms, the scent cone rises; scent from warm objects or warm areas rises in cool or cold air. It is best to work the dog above low areas so he can detect the rising scent. In the evening, the opposite takes place and the scent travels down or rises a little and then returns to the ground. This is the best time to use a dog since the most scent is available at ground level. It is

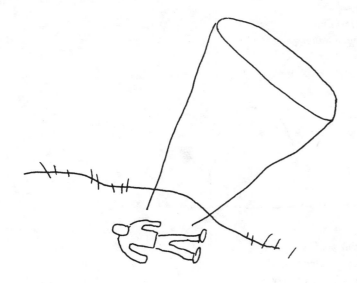

An example of how the scent cone from a person rises and spreads. Drawing by Joseph T. McNichol.

Much like water, scent will flow down a slope, following a path of least resistance. Drawing by Joseph T. McNichol.

Scent can rise from its source, return to the ground forming a scent pool, rise again and fall. This is called looping. Drawing by Joseph T. McNichol.

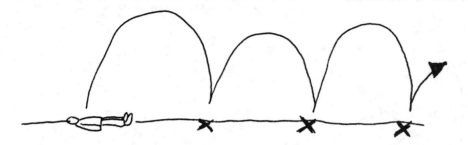

When scent loops, the dog may miss some of the scent pools and find others. By determining the wind direction and pattern of alerts, you can determine from which direction the source of scent is most likely coming. Drawing by Joseph T. McNichol.

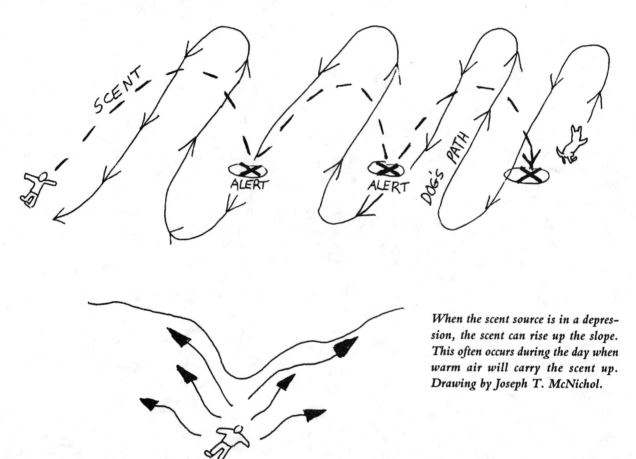

When the scent source is in a depression, the scent can rise up the slope. This often occurs during the day when warm air will carry the scent up. Drawing by Joseph T. McNichol.

also best to work the dog in the low areas to catch the scent from the victim above you. If there is a cold layer of air with warm air beneath, the conditions that cause smog alerts and smoke to hang around in the air, the scent also rises and lingers. If a dog is working on flat ground, he may have difficulty detecting the scent, but if he detects scent on a hill or mountain and loses it above and below the scent band, it is good to check with the other dog teams working at the same level to see if they are experiencing the same thing. If so, the combination of Alerts can point out the direction to the source of the scent. If a victim is hidden long enough and scent pooling takes place (little or no breeze to move the scent around), the scent pool can saturate the area, making it difficult for the dog to locate the source of the scent.

Sometimes, there will not be much of a scent pool for the dog to detect, causing the dog to miss it entirely. When a victim is very still, as when the person is sleeping or passed out, he gives off much less scent than when he is moving. Also, scent availability is determined by the amount of exposed body. Thus, a person who has taken shelter, either in a plastic bag, space blanket, buried in the snow, under branches (especially leafy branches) and has fallen asleep, gives off a very small scent pool, even if he remains in one place for a while. In such situations, it is up to the dog handler to investigate areas in which a person could be hidden, or specifically send the dog into those areas.

As scent travels over an area, the terrain features can cause dead spaces to form where no scent has been carried. These dead spaces are in tucked-away areas the wind has bypassed. A dead area might be at the base of a sheer cliff where the wind blew off the top of the cliff and angled down, missing the base. Another dead space is where a strong breeze has blown the scent over a depression instead of into it. If the dog is following a scent and loses it, this could be the result of a dead space. Move on and try to pick up the scent again.

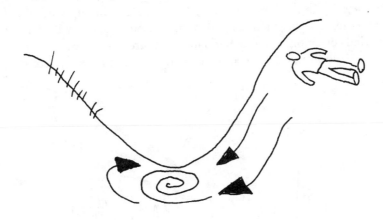

Scent can travel down a slope and collect in a low area. The highest concentration of scent will be in the scent pool in the low area. Drawing by Joseph T. McNichol.

The way scent travels and its availability depend on the weather, terrain, age of the scent trail and source, the condition of the scent source, the air flow, wind, vegetation, concealment of the source, and time of day you are searching. The combination of all these factors makes each situation unique. It is up to the dog handler to determine the conditions so he can understand how his dog reacts in various situations. Most important, the handler must analyze each situation to decide what his dog is communicating to him so he can direct his dog to lead him to the victim. The dog and handler are a team, each with his specific job and expertise.

Test the Wind

When training for SAR work, it is important always to know what the wind is doing and which way it is blowing. Many exercises presented later in this book require you to test the wind. There are a number of ways to do this, and you should be able to use all of them. The easiest way to check the wind constantly is to use a *Bic*-type lighter. By watching the flame, which responds to the slightest breeze, you can determine which way the wind is blowing. When you test the wind, always test at eye level and again at the dog's nose level. In certain conditions and terrain, the wind will be different at each level.

Another way to test the wind is to use the small smoke bombs that are available for about 25 cents each. This is the most effective method to check how the wind is blowing from your victim to the dog. After the dog has found your training victim, have the victim light a smoke bomb and watch what the smoke does in relation to where the dog was working. It will help you understand what scent was available to the dog.

Another method employs a small, compressible object filled with powder. The device used to clean an infant's nose is good, or find something you can squeeze to expel a burst of powder into the air. Yet another method is to tie sewing thread around your finger or wrist, allowing enough to hang down to see which way the wind is blowing.

In disasters when it is not safe to use a lighter, use methods that are okay around flammable conditions. Whatever method you use, check the wind.

As a rule, the SAR dog handler works a dog perpendicular to the direction of the wind. This gives the dog the best advantage to pick up an available scent cone. By tracking the dog's Alerts, you can determine from which direction the scent is coming—providing your dog is going upwind (the dog is facing into the wind). With a steady breeze, working your dog upwind, you can accurately detect the source of the scent. However, in variable wind conditions and rough terrain, the source of the scent can be difficult to determine. In a variable wind, you can double grid an area, reducing the size of the search sector.

Both man-made and natural obstacles can cause the scent to eddy and swirl. Drawing by Joseph T. McNichol.

WIND DIRECTION

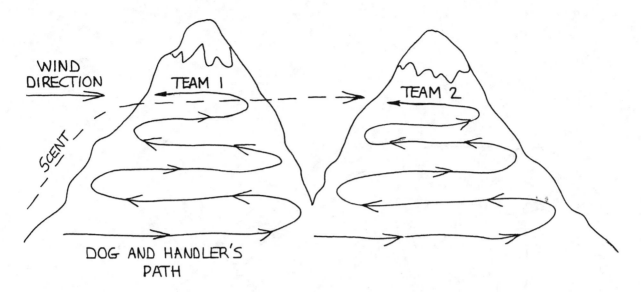

Cold air above and warm air below can cause a scent band to form. The dog will hit on the scent in the scent band. By recording the alerts of different teams working along the scent band, the Incident Commander will be able to determine where to concentrate the search effort. Drawing by Joseph T. McNichol.

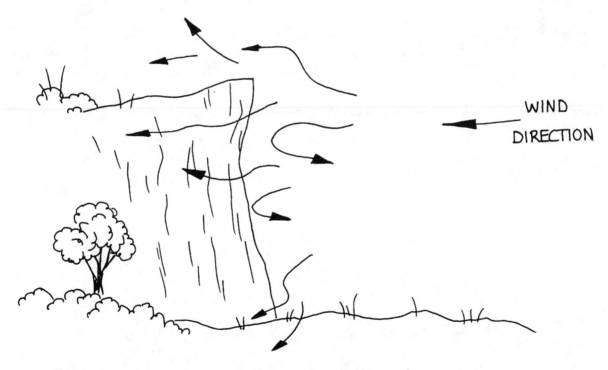

If the wind is blowing into an obstruction (man-made or natural), the scent can be scattered. Drawing by Joseph T. McNichol.

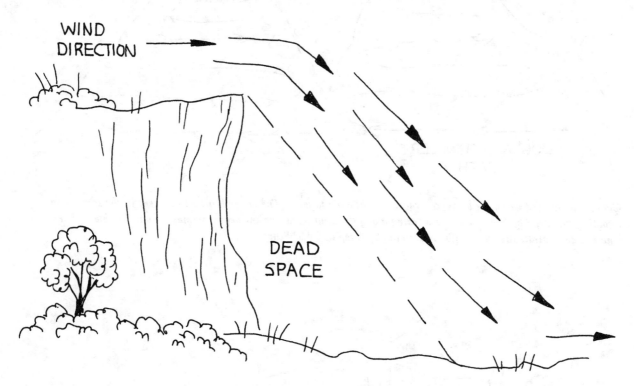

When scent is carried over land features that drop suddenly, there can be a dead space next to the drop. Drawing by Joseph T. McNichol.

PART II
TRAINING THE SEARCH AND RESCUE DOG

Chapter 7
Airscenting

Wilderness Training

NOTE: For all airscenting problems (except Levels 1 and 2) whether the dog is allowed to see the victim leave or not, encourage the dog to airscent and not trail or track. If the track of the victim is always in front of the dog, some dogs will only track and will tend not to airscent. A good search dog will use all of his senses to find the victim and put his nose where the scent is, regardless of whether it means tracking, trailing, or airscenting.

To set up an exercise so it is not always a tracking problem, arrange that the dog runs in a different place from the track of the victim. Have the dog approach the spot from a different direction from the way the victim came to it.

Also, before you start your SAR training, read the section on the Alert. Teach your dog the mechanics of the Alert before the dog must use them.

The Victim

The helper who is portraying the victim is a key person who can make your SAR dog training succeed or fail. This is especially true in the beginning stages of training. It is the victim's job to keep the dog's interest. The dog should be so interested in the victim that more than anything he wants to go and see where the victim went and what the victim is doing. The timing of the victim's response to the dog is also critical. If the victim does not understand what he is doing, it is important for you to explain carefully what to do and to use someone who can follow directions well. Without a good victim you cannot have a successful training session.

Equally important is the level of praise the dog must receive from both the victim and handler. Many SAR dog handlers believe the most important praise is the praise that comes from the victim since this motivates the dog to find the victim. No one disagrees that the SAR dog must receive a great deal of praise for his work. The amount required will vary with each dog. Some people tend to be very low key. This may result in a low-key, unmotivated dog.

The Observer

The observer, or spotter, is critical for the success of a water, cadaver or disaster search. In some situations, you will want more than one observer placed strategically to pinpoint Alert locations by triangulation. The observer acts as a safety officer to watch for dangers that might not be apparent to the SAR dog handler and other rescue personnel. The observer also looks for any subtle body language the SAR dog may give that the handler can miss.

Ranging

As you progress through the levels of wilderness training, you want to encourage your dog to range, searching the area around you for scent. How far the dog works from you depends on the problem, the density of the brush, and the terrain you are working. The idea of using the dog is to cover more ground faster than possible without a dog. The dog is also able to get into and reach places not readily accessible to a human.

Ideally, the dog ranges in a circle around the handler when off-leash, and back and forth in front of the handler when on-leash. The dog can also work a semicircle around the handler off-leash in the same manner a flushing dog looks for birds or a herding dog weaves back and forth to keep stock bunched up. In certain situations, the dog may walk close and ahead of the handler and not range at all. This method requires the handler to cover more ground than when the dog is covering much of the ground. In all ranging, the goal is to have the dog work across the wind to catch any available scent. Some people don't want the dog to check back too often; it wastes the dog's energy. Other handlers, however, want their dogs to keep in touch. An occasional check-back from the dog is fine.

Often, a dog will range too far. This is especially true for young dogs who are full of excitement and energy. You never want the dog too far away from you; you may lose track of the dog, or he may go out of hearing range (in the event he is taught to wait and bark when he has found something). If the dog is too far from you and you are not sure in which direction he has headed, you would have difficulty finding the dog if he were injured. Also, if you depend on a natural Alert, you will miss the Alert and other subtle Alerts the dog may give. Therefore, how visible the dog is and how far he ranges depends in large part on how you work the dog.

If the dog ranges too far, you can correct him by hiding from the dog. He will come back to see where you are and not be able to find you right away. This action communicates that he must stay closer and check in on you more often. If this method does not work, wait until the dog is far ahead and backtrack from the spot where the dog last saw you. Your dog should become anxious and follow you. Again, he will get the message to stay closer. Another way to teach the dog to range closer is to call him back whenever he gets too far ahead of you. Just as the dog reaches the limit you have set, recall the dog or give the dog a command to wait, praise him for waiting or returning to you, and send him out again. By repeating this often enough, the dog will learn to judge how far he can go. However, you must be very careful not to discourage a dog who is hot on a scent or following through on an Alert. Do not depend on yourself to see every Alert your dog gives. Every handler makes mistakes and misreads his dog at some time. One way to avoid putting the limits on a dog who is ranging too far is to be sure that there is no victim for the dog to find. Train the dog to limit his range as a separate exercise.

Snow search in Washington State by Marcia Koenig's dog Bear. Photo courtesy of Marcia Koenig.

The dog who stays too close must be encouraged to leave you to look for scent. Place a victim just beyond the dog's natural ranging distance. It is also helpful to have two-way radios so you can let the victim know when to assist. When the dog reaches the point where he starts to return to you, have the victim call the dog's name while you encourage the dog to find the victim. If the dog hesitates at any point, have the victim make a moaning noise or call the dog. As the dog leaves you to find the victim, you should allow the dog to go on his own and not follow closely. This encourges the dog to leave you to go to the victim. Once the dog reaches the victim he can either be rewarded or return to you for the Alert and re-find as he has been taught. Reward the dog with a Find (allowing him to find a victim) for leaving you.

A dog may stay too close because you talk to him too much. You may not realize you are doing this, so it helps to ask someone to watch and listen while you work. Once you give the dog the command to search, do not talk to the dog unless he needs extra encouragement or direction.

One way to teach the dog how to loop around you or to range back and forth in front of you is to zigzag back and forth yourself. As the dog gets the idea, you can decrease your zigzags until the dog continues to work a pattern while you walk in a straight line.

LEVEL 1: BEGINNER RUNAWAY

GOAL: To teach the dog the command to find his human victim.

OBJECTIVE: To have the dog follow his handler to a hiding place.

METHOD:
Unless you are sure the dog will not run off or wander, this exercise should be worked on-leash. The dog should be kept on-leash so the assistant can maintain complete control over the dog at all times. For a well-socialized, people-loving dog, it is not necessary for the assistant to be someone the dog knows. However, if the dog is shy, insecure, or not comfortable with the assistant, the dog should become acquainted with the assistant first. Allow the assistant and dog to play a number of times prior to the training session. The assistant should not be someone the dog feels either uncomfortable with or so comfortable that he does not want to leave the assistant to go find his handler. At this stage, it is important for the dog to have a strong bond with his handler. If you are starting a new pup, give him a few weeks to bond prior to starting his training.

The main goal is to teach the dog that when he is given the Find command, he is to look for a human. Start training in an area that is reasonably open with brush or objects for a person to hide behind. Be sure the wind is coming toward the dog carrying the scent of the handler into the dog's face (see Wind, Scent and Dog: The Nature of Scent). The assistant holds the dog while the handler stands in front of the dog. The handler runs away from the dog and ducks behind an object while the dog watches. The runaway should be within about 50 and 100 feet of the dog to begin with. The purpose of the exercise is to keep the dog focused on the handler as he is running away and to entice the dog to chase the handler. To do this, the handler should jump, call the dog's name and make noise.

The exercise must be kept very short so the dog does not lose interest. If the dog loses interest, make the runaway shorter until you find the distance at which the dog can maintain a high level of curiosity. While the handler is jumping around and calling the dog, the assistant excites the dog by saying things such as, "Where's he going? Where's he going?" The instant the handler is out of sight, the assistant runs with the dog to the handler, giving the Find command as they run. Keep in mind, the dog should be able to see where the handler ducked behind the brush. The Find is visual because the main point of the exercise is to teach the dog the Find concept and command, not to develop the dog's search skill.

When the dog reaches the handler, reward him with whatever he likes best. Ideally, this is a game, but food can be included if it is needed to motivate the dog. If you use food, be sure to make the game the primary

WIND DIRECTION

Beginner runaway: the assistant runs from the dog in such a manner as to keep the dog's attention while hiding. Drawing by Joseph T. McNichol.

The Bringsel type of Alert. Drawing by Joseph T. McNichol.

The Bringsel is an adjustable piece of leather attached to the collar. When the dog finds a victim, he will pick up the leather object and carry it to his handler. Drawing by Joseph T. McNichol.

reward by focusing on the game rather than the food. As soon as the game is sufficient, the food reward can be discontinued.

This exercise is continued until the dog is excited and barks and pulls to go find the handler. When it is clear from the dog's anticipation that he knows and likes the game of finding his handler, you are ready to go on to the next level. Remember, the dog should show anticipation consistently to illustrate he knows the exercise. It usually takes five to seven sessions, one a day, for a dog to transfer a lesson to his long term memory. Because this exercise is the foundation of the Find concept, do not rush the dog, especially if he is under one year of age.

In some cases, the dog will not need a visual Find. Some handlers say they do not want the dog to have a visual Find since the dog must be weaned from it later. If you agree, set up the problem in the same manner except do not allow the dog to see the victim run away. With a nonvisual problem, the victim should run away in a half circle to the hiding place up-wind from the dog. It is important that the dog always "wins" by finding his victim and that the exercise ends on a high note.

PROBLEMS:

If the dog is very young, he may not run right into the handler's hiding place, especially if the handler is partially hidden in brush. If this happens, the handler calls the dog and encourages the dog to come to him. If the handler has developed a play routine with the dog, he can use the play object (stick, ball, etc.) to lure the dog to him. Food can also be used as a lure. If the dog comes to the hiding place, the handler and handler immediately reward the dog with the lure. If the dog refuses, but stands his ground and looks at the handler, the handler comes out to the dog immediately and praises him. If the dog backs away from the handler, the handler stoops down and calls the dog while the assistant encourages the dog to go to the handler. As soon as the dog and handler are together, the assistant and handler reward the dog.

If the dog refuses to come in to the handler after the second try, the exercise should be discontinued immediately. The dog may not be bonded enough to the handler, or may be too shy to handle the excitement. At this point, the SAR training must stop and the handler should focus his efforts on socializing the dog, developing a stronger bond and building the dog's confidence through basic obedience work. Once the handler believes the dog has progressed, he can try SAR work again. If the dog does not like to do the work, the handler can wait until the dog matures and try again. If an older dog refuses to work, the same method should be used to encourage him as mentioned above. If it does not produce results, the dog may not be SAR material.

Remember, very young dogs (6 to 12 weeks old) do not have enough life experience to handle strange situations. This is why careful socialization is important.

TEST: Level 1

Set the test in an open area with light brush or objects.

There should be something to hide behind no more than 100 feet away. The wind should be blowing toward the dog.

With the dog on-leash, the assistant holds the dog while the handler runs away, making noise while he is running to attract the dog. At the same time, the assistant encourages the dog to look at the handler. The dog should watch the handler and strain to go and find him. As soon as the handler hides, the assistant gives the dog the Find command and runs with the dog to the handler. Both the assistant and the handler praise the dog. The dog should indicate by his excitement and desire to find his handler that he understands the exercise. The dog runs to the hiding place with no hesitation.

GOAL: To reinforce the command to find a human victim.

OBJECTIVE: To have the dog find someone other than his handler or a family member.

METHOD:

This exercise is the same as Level 1. The distance for the runaway is between 50 to 100 feet. The wind is blowing from the victim to the dog. The handler holds the dog and the assistant (ideally the same one who handled the dog for Level 1) runs away from the dog and ducks behind an object. While the assistant is running away, he should get and keep the dog's attention as in Level 1. The handler encourages the dog to pay attention to the assistant by using the same questions as in Level 1: "Where's he going, where's he going?" As soon as the assistant ducks out of sight, the handler gives the dog the Find command and runs with the dog after the assistant. The handler allows the dog to reach the assistant (victim) first. The assistant plays with the dog before the handler approaches. After the dog has a play period with the assistant (or victim), the handler can join in or take over the play reward. Again, the Find is primarily visual. The main objective is to reinforce the Find command and teach the dog to find humans.

Once the dog shows enthusiasm for finding someone not related to the family, you are ready to go on to the next level.

PROBLEMS:

The dog may be reluctant to go in to the victim. Using the same techniques as outlined in Level 1, encourage the dog to go in to the victim by either leading him in, or by luring him in with the stick, ball, or food reward. Give the victim the lure and tease the dog with it the moment he hesitates to go in to the victim. The handler should encourage the dog to go in to the victim by calling the dog and moving in the direction of the victim. It is not a good idea to force the dog in to the victim. This may frighten the dog, causing him to pull away in confusion.

As soon as the dog gets close enough to the victim to see the lure or reward, the victim can extend his hand and offer the reward. At this time, the victim and handler should praise and play with the dog. Once the dog sees there is nothing to fear, he should quickly get over his hesitancy to go in to the victim. If the dog does not get over his fear after two or three tries, go back to Level 1 for a few weeks. When the dog is working confidently at Level 1, try Level 2 again. If the dog still does not go boldly into his victim, he may not be suited for SAR work. It is important for the dog to like the work in order to go on to the next levels of training.

If the dog has been trained for personal protection work, it is essential at Level 2 to teach the dog he is not allowed to "hit" or bite his victim. At this level, make it very clear to the dog that there is a big difference between SAR work and personal protection work. It is important that the commands for SAR work sound very different from the commands for bite work. You will need a confident victim who will give the dog a loud No or other corrective sound, and, if necessary, correct the dog if he gets mouthy.

As the excitement builds, the timing of the reward and play is essential. The victim can sit facing the dog with a tug toy held motionless against his chest for the dog's play reward. You may want to keep some dogs on a long leash for control until you are comfortable about the lesson and the dog's desire to bite. However, with a good victim you should be able to do this off-leash.

TEST: Level 2

Set the test in an open area with light brush or objects to hide behind. The victim runs into the wind, with the wind blowing toward the dog. With the dog on-leash, the handler holds the dog, encouraging the dog

WIND DIRECTION

VICTIM'S PATH

Intermediate runaway: The assistant quietly walks away and hides,
taking care not to walk in a straight line from the dog to the hiding place.
Drawing by Joseph T. McNichol.

to watch the victim run away. The victim attracts the dog's attention by making noises and calling to the dog. The victim ducks behind an object or brush 50 to 100 feet away. As soon as the victim is hidden, the handler gives the dog the Find command and lets the dog run to the victim. The handler can follow along after the dog has had a chance to play with the victim. This keeps the dog from becoming too dependent on the handler and keeps focus on the victim. The dog should show a high level of excitement as soon as the victim starts to run away. The dog should pull the handler in an effort to get to the victim. Upon reaching the site where the victim is hidden, the dog goes right in to the victim in friendly manner and shows joy at finding him.

LEVEL 3: INTERMEDIATE RUNAWAY

GOAL: To solidify the dog's desire to find a human victim.

OBJECTIVE: To teach the dog to find a victim when delayed.

METHOD:
A nonfamily member acts as the victim; the best victim is someone the dog does not know very well. The

Rapelling down a vertical incline with a German Shepherd in harness. Drawing by Marcus Adkins.

setting is the same as Level 2. This exercise is performed with the dog on-leash unless the dog is off-leash obedience trained. The victim runs away without calling the dog or focusing the dog's attention on himself in any manner. The handler stands quietly and lets the dog watch the victim walk away. Once the victim is in place, encourage the dog a little by saying, "Where is he? Where is he?" Wait for one or two minutes before sending the dog to find the victim. As the dog progresses at this level, gradually increase the time the dog waits (not more than five minutes). To encourage the dog to airscent, be sure the victim has moved into the area from a different direction from the dog. When you cover the area, make the dog search quarters in a grid pattern. The dog may become confused as to how and where he should search. Show the dog how to search in a grid by walking the grid pattern yourself as you encourage the dog to range. When he hits the scent cone, he will catch on to what searching is all about.

PROBLEMS:

A very young or immature dog may not have a long attention span and may not be able to keep his mind on the task for the five-minute delay. Dogs who are three or four months old should be able to handle the five-minute delay. If not, they should not be pushed. Work to increase the dog's attention by gradually adding seconds and minutes to the level the dog can handle, or tease the dog after two minutes by having the victim make a noise or call to the dog.

TEST: Level 3

Set the test in an open area with a light breeze blowing from the victim to the dog. The area should provide adequate cover for a victim to hide easily.

The dog and handler wait quietly while the victim walks away to hide no more than 100 feet from the dog. The handler waits five minutes before sending the dog to find the victim. The dog need not maintain a high level of excitement (jumping and barking) during the five-minute wait but should show enthusiasm (intently watching the victim go away and illustrating he wants to go too) while the victim walks away. When given the Find command, the dog will run right in to the victim without hesitation. The dog does not wander more than 20 feet or so off the victim's path. While it is okay for the dog to cast back and forth, he should not run all over the place as if on a lark; he should be focused on finding the victim.

LEVEL 4: ADVANCED RUNAWAY

GOAL: To reinforce the Find command for finding a nonfamily member, and to heighten the dog's anticipation and drive to perform the Find.

OBJECTIVE: To have the dog work off-leash and find his victim without seeing the victim run away.

METHOD:

Start this exercise with the dog on-leash. The victim (not a family member) hides about 100 feet from the starting point. Be sure the wind is blowing from the victim to the dog. Do not excite the dog as in Level 1 and 2 with statements such as, "Where is he going?" Do not let the dog watch the victim go away. As soon as the victim is hiding and ready, give the dog the Find command and go with the dog as he leads you in to the victim. Both you and the victim should praise the dog as soon as he finds the victim.

As the dog successfully finds his victim, increase the search area. Also, start allowing the dog work off-leash. At this point, it is important for you to know where your victim is and when he is ready to be found. This usually means you and the victim must use hand-held radios for communication. Do not allow the victim to make an audio signal (such as a whistle) to let you know he is ready because the dog will pick up on this and will not search with his nose. When your dog can work well off-leash, you can encourage him to range and work the area in a grid pattern. Once he hits the scent cone while working his grid, he will learn to range and work the wind in his favor without being told. At times, you may have to prompt the dog to enter brush and work difficult areas instead of going around or avoiding them. Now is also the time to start to practice and use basic directional commands. However, this is not the time to teach directional commands.

PROBLEMS:

The dog could miss his victim. At this point, finding the victim means the dog must use his sense of smell. Many conditions affect scent: time of day, weather conditions, time of year, humidity, contaminating odors, distracting odors, etc. Depending on the weather conditions, the scent could be looping, blowing in an erratic manner, going straight up and so on. The dog could miss the victim because the scent cone from the victim is not available for him to find; therefore, you must be aware of how the scent is blowing (see Wind, Scent and Dog). The dog could also miss his victim because he does not have an interest in doing the work, or his nose is not good enough to find the victim.

The dog could show interest in animal scents and not follow the human scent. If this happens, it must be corrected right away. If it is just a passing interest, redirect the dog away from the animal smell and back to the task of finding the victim by telling the dog No when he sniffs the animal scent and giving the dog the Find command. To avoid confusing the dog, you must be 100 percent certain when you give the dog a No that he is following animal scent and not human scent. A sure indication is if he finds a den, hole, or animal droppings. Do not assume that because your victim was not in the area that there is no human scent. Someone else could have walked through the area before you. On a real search, it is not unusual for a victim to follow an animal trail, since this may be the only path available. This means you must have strong faith in your dog that he is not just following animal scent. If the dog does not respond to this simple No, read the section on Game Chasing.

A dog may find his victim and then take off. If this happens, put the dog back on-leash. It is important that the victim make himself interesting to the dog. He can use a toy, teasing, food, or whatever turns the dog on. If the dog does not come when called, reinforce his obedience work. For this problem, the handler should not be so far behind the dog that he cannot see or control him. If this is the case, reduce the distance between the handler and victim.

TEST: Level 4

Set the test in light brush, in a relatively open area with the breeze blowing from victim to dog. The victim, a stranger to the dog, hides between 100 to 200 feet from the starting point. The dog does not see the victim hide. When the victim is in place, the handler gives the dog the start exercise signal and then the Find command. The dog runs immediately in the direction the victim traveled or grids the area in an effort to find the scent cone. When the dog finds the victim, he goes in to the victim without hesitation. If the dog shows little or no interest, wanders off before or after finding the victim, or hesitates to go into the victim, the handler should go back a level or two until the dog does not hesitate. At this point in the training, the handler should observe the dog carefully to decide if the dog has the nose and interest for SAR work. The dog must start to rely upon his nose to find the victim.

Airlifting a Beauceron. Drawing by Nina Bondarenko.

Beauceron finding a child in a wilderness search. Drawing by Nina Bondarenko.

LEVEL 5: BEGINNING THE RE-FIND

NOTE: To avoid future problems and ensure a proper response from the dog, he must go directly in to the victim, return directly to you and lead you right to the victim. Do not allow the dog to stop, wander or play during the exercise. If your dog is not obedient enough to work off-leash, do not continue until your dog is able to be controlled off leash, or use a long leash. However, some handlers do not like to use a long leash because the leash can become a crutch and the dog will not work in a reliable fashion without it. Training with a long leash must be done very carefully to avoid this. If a dog is not excited or interested enough in SAR work to work without a leash, it could indicate that the dog has not been properly motivated to find his victim or that the dog has no real desire to do the work.

GOAL: To train the dog to return to you after he has found the victim.

OBJECTIVE: The dog must now return to you to earn his reward instead of getting his reward immediately upon finding the victim.

METHOD:

Set up the problem the same as Level 4. Send the dog out to find the victim, but stop about halfway between the starting point and the victim. The victim ignores the dog when the dog reaches him instead of praising the dog as before. Key in this exercise is knowing exactly when the dog has found the victim. You and the victim work with hand-held radios. When using radios, the victim quietly lets you know when the dog has found him (while ignoring the dog). Working in an open area with light brush is ideal because you can see when the dog finds the victim while the victim stays absolutely still. As soon as the dog goes in to the victim and makes contact, call the dog back. When the dog returns to you, praise the dog in the same manner as you did for finding the victim. The victim does not come out and praise the dog at this point.

PROBLEMS:

1. The dog may not return to you when called, but stays with the victim. If this happens, get very close to the victim while calling the dog to get the dog to focus on you. If the dog makes a slight move to go to you, praise the dog and go in to the victim, at which time both you and the victim praise the dog. Most of the praise should be from the victim. Also work on obedience with the dog. You can try three additional lessons to teach this exercise to the dog.

The handler squats down or goes behind a tree or other object. The dog seeks out the handler if the dog has strongly bonded with him. Once the dog comes to the handler, tell the dog Show Me and act happy and excited. The dog leads the handler back to the victim and both parties give the dog lots of praise and reward.

Put the dog on a long line and work the dog through the problem. After the dog has found the victim, coax the dog to you. Take care to keep the long leash from being tangled. Do not use a leash jerk or abusive punishment when calling the dog, since the dog could interpret the correction to mean he should not go in to the victim or he is not to come to you. If the dog does not readily come when he is called and gently coaxed, shorten the distance between you, the dog, and the victim to the point where the dog feels you are in control. The dog may wish to stay with the victim because he expects praise from the victim. If this is the case, the victim should ignore the dog when he is found. Initially, the dog may be confused, but he should quickly catch on. Do not use the long line more than a few times. Voice control, motivation, and bonding are the key elements which make this exercise work best.

Initiate the Go To exercise

2. The dog may find the victim and then go off in pursuit of animal scents or just wander. This usually happens because the victim was not interesting enough or the dog thinks the exercise is finished once he has found the victim. The same methods as above should correct this problem. However, if the dog is more

interested in finding animals and consistently follows animal scent, proof your dog against this. (See the section on Game Chasing.). Sometimes it is only necessary to reinforce the desirable behavior. Motivate your dog more than in previous training sessions. A food or more enthusiastic play reward may do the trick. Again, work the dog on the long line to maintain control at adistance. When the dog moves toward you, praise him. If he turns away from you, tell him No. When he reaches you, get excited and happy, give the dog lots of verbal praise, pats, and a tidbit of food.

TEST: Level 5

Set the test in light brush or woods with the breeze blowing toward the dog from the victim. The victim hides about 100 to 200 feet from the starting point. The dog is not allowed to see the victim go and hide. As soon as the victim is ready, bring the dog to the starting point and give the Find command. The dog should show enthusiasm for the exercise and rush to find the victim. As soon as the dog makes contact with the victim, he should go in to the victim without hesitation, and then should immediately return to the handler.

Beginning Re-Find: The dog is encouraged to find the victim and return to the handler. Drawing by Joseph T. McNichol.

Chapter 8
The Alert

General Principles

The Alert, a signal the dog gives you to let you know he has found someone, is one of the more controversial aspects of SAR dog work. Many handlers have different ideas about what the Alert should be and how the Alert should be done. Most trainers agree, however, that the Alert should be readable in all conditions. This includes situations in which you cannot either see the dog very well (at night for example) or hear the dog (such as in windy or noisy locations). There are also different Alerts for different types of SAR work. Each specialized Alert is covered in the section on that training, i.e. disaster, avalanche, water, etc.

The Alert you choose is limited only by your imagination. Whatever works and meets the criteria is okay. To determine which Alert to use, pick one that comes naturally to your dog. For example, retrievers may work best with a retrieve Alert. The working breeds may respond best to a body contact Alert. Watch your dog and try to determine if he has some special mannerism that would work well as an Alert.

No matter what Alert you decide to use, you still have to learn the natural Alert (Method 7). Most of the clearly defined Alerts are used when the dog finds something tangible, such as the victim, an article of clothing, or an object. But many times, the dog will not find physical evidence, only scent. You must be able to read your dog so well that you can tell if he has found some scent, however slight. A dog should not bypass weak scent. When the dog finds weak scent, he will not give the primary or strong Alert without training, but will give a natural Alert. Learn to read his natural Alert.

The False Alert

One of the most important aspects of teaching your dog the Alert is to avoid the false Alert. Often in his enthusiasm to have the dog perform correctly and find the victim, a handler will unconsciously signal his dog to go in to a victim or to give an Alert. Sometimes a dog will pick up on this signal and give an Alert even though the victim was not found. This is a false Alert. To avoid this, be sure to give your dog enough time to work out the problem. Encourage him only when necessary and just enough to get the job done.

If the handler always knows where the victim is hiding, the dog may never find the victim on his own. He may never be able to find a real victim. One good way to check for hidden signals is to ask someone who knows working dogs to watch you work with your dog. They should watch for unconscious acts, such as pointing in the correct direction when sending a dog to find a victim. Another common mistake is to cue the dog for an Alert every time the dog returns after a Find. While you have to cue the dog to teach him to give the Alert at first, you must do it as infrequently as possible.

LEVEL 1: ALERT

GOAL: To teach the dog to give you a persistent signal or Alert to let you know he has found his victim.

OBJECTIVE: To train the dog, after he has found his victim and returned to you, to give you a recognizable Alert.

Method 1: Bark Alert Type 1

The Bark Alert is convenient because it is easy to teach and does not require any equipment. Prior to search training, teach the dog to Speak on command. As soon as the dog comes to you to let you know he has found his victim, give him the speak command and a food reward or pat with a hearty Good Dog. Repeat the exercise until the dog returns and barks without being told.

Method 2: Bark Alert Type 2

This method uses the Bark Alert without the Re-find. The dog stays with the victim (either sitting or lying down next to the victim) and barks continuously until the handler arrives. While this method may sound good and is often used in Europe, it has limitations in vast wilderness settings. The dog must be trained to work close so you hear him clearly enough to determine the direction of the bark. In areas of vast forest and mountains, a dog who must work very close can lengthen the time it takes to search an area. There will also be search conditions in which your ability to hear will be limited by wind, by hats, or by loud noises, such as white water. Another consideration is that the tired dog must continue to bark while he waits for you to reach him. Barking continuously is exhausting. In the wilderness, many dogs will bark for awhile and then go back to check on the handler because they want their reward. Some handlers teach the Bark Alert for victims who are not accessible, as in a disaster, and to do a Re-find in situations where the dog can reach the victim.

For the Bark Alert, train your dog to the search level just prior to the Re-find. Instead of doing a Re-find, teach the dog to wait by the victim and bark. When the dog reaches the victim, have the victim give the dog the Speak command. Once the dog speaks, run in and praise the dog. The victim should also praise the dog. Another way to teach the dog to bark at the victim is to have the victim tease the dog with food or a toy. This works best when the victim is not readily accessible to the dog. (See the Disaster Alert for Buried Victims.)

Method 3: Bark Alert Type 3

This Alert combines both Method 1 and 2. The dog barks when he finds his victim, then returns to the handler and barks again. To teach this, do the Re-find, teach the dog to bark when he reaches the victim, and to bark again when he returns to the handler. It is just a matter of adding a step to the Alert sequence.

Method 4: Other Physical Alert Signals

Any other Alert that involves a signal should be taught in the same manner. If you want your dog to jump on you or hit you with his paw (in the way hearing-ear dogs alert their handlers), first teach the dog the actual signal in a separate lesson. Then incorporate it into search training. Some types of signals may be trouble to initiate. In this case, wait for the signal to occur naturally and praise the dog for the behavior as you name it with the command.

Some other signals include a body bang—the dog bumps you with his shoulder, jumps on you, or hits you with his paws; or the pull—the dog grabs your clothing or a special tug device and pulls gently or takes your hand or arm in his mouth. Remember, be inventive but be careful. Some dogs like to pick up objects such as sticks as a signal. This is a problem in contaminated areas. It is a good idea to always carry a safe object for the dog to pick up, such as a tug toy, ball, etc.

Method 5: Retrieve or Bringsel

The bringsel is an adjustable piece of leather attached by a snap to the dog's collar. The bringsel Alert was used during the Second World War by Red Cross dogs and is well-tried. For this method, the dog must first master the retrieve. He should know the Fetch, Take-it and Hold-it commands prior to SAR training. The dog must already feel comfortable with the bringsel, both in carrying the bringsel in retrieve games and having it hang from his collar.

The victim takes the bringsel when he hides about 50 feet away. When the victim gets in place, he puts the bringsel on the ground next to him in plain sight and within easy reach. The handler gives the dog the Find command and follows the dog to the victim, but does not go in to the victim when the dog does. Stay about 30 feet away. As soon as the dog finds the victim, who totally ignores the dog, give the dog the Fetch command. If the dog does not go for the bringsel, the victim can tease the dog with the bringsel just enough to call attention to it. The dog should return with the bringsel in his mouth. Once the dog is doing this reliably, attach the bringsel to the collar and repeat the exercise.

If the dog is reluctant to pick up the bringsel when it is attached to the collar, the victim should wiggle it back and forth to call the dog's attention to it. The moment the dog makes the slightest move to nose the bringsel, give the command to Fetch again. As soon as the dog picks up the bringsel, give a Come command. This stage of the exercise should be repeated until the dog automatically picks up the bringsel when he finds his victim and returns to the handler.

Sometimes using two bringsels encourages the dog to pick one up. The victim has the first bringsel and teases the dog with it as he runs away. The dog has another bringsel attached to the collar. When the dog reaches the victim, the victim can tease the dog with the attached bringsel and encourages the dog to play with it until the dog takes the second bringsel in his mouth.

Variations of this Alert can be used with objects that are not attached to the dog: balls, sticks, towels, articles of clothing, etc. Whatever is used should always be available to the dog when he finds the victim. Some handlers wear a hand towel or keep a bandana in their pockets for dogs to grab when they return as their Alerts. Some handlers let the dogs pick up any objects near the victims and bring them as Alerts. This has limitations and can present a frustrating problem to the dog if nothing is readily available. A dog may try to pick up a log for want of a stick. The mechanics of the retrieve must be taught before you reach this stage of training. (See Additional Commands: The Article.)

Method 6: Alert Object

This method is similar to the retrieve Alert except it does not require that the dog bring you an object. Instead, the dog returns to you to play with an object you have on your person. The play session should be short. The main purpose of play is to focus the dog's attention on the object that is his reward, and to encourage the dog to request the object as his Alert, signaling that he has found the victim.

Many SAR handlers use play as the primary reward for the dog after the entire search exercise is completed. Play is a different activity from the Alert. You must be careful when a play activity is used as an Alert, such as tug-of-war or fetch games, since you can easily confuse spontaneous play behavior with an Alert. To reduce this confusion, allow the Alert behavior only when the dog makes a Find. For example, if you allow your dog to grab a tug toy when he returns to you as his Alert, he must only have the tug toy available to him during training or an actual search. He cannot play with it other times. The dog must be able to make a clear distinction between his Alert object and a play reward after he has completed the entire search exercise.

Method 7: Natural Alert

The natural Alert requires close observation of your dog as he works his search problems. You must learn to read your dog to know when he has detected a scent. He will act differently, either by holding his ears in a different manner, by a certain walk, usually a zigzag back and forth, or he may dance in excitement. Some dogs have subtle natural Alerts while others are so obvious anyone can read them. You must learn to read your dog whether you teach clearly defined Alerts or not. In most cases, the younger the dog, the more difficult he is to read because young dogs tend to work more quickly. As they get the hang of the training and settle down, you can usually read the dog's Alert much better.

Jib, a Border Collie, giving a jump alert or body Bang BANG Alert.

Jib leading handler to a victim.

Scout giving a bark alert.

Jib leading his handler to a victim on a Re-Find.

TEST: Level 1

Set the test in light brush or woods with a breeze blowing from the victim to the starting point. The victim should be well hidden. The area should be large enough for the dog to work the problem out.

After the victim is in place, bring the dog to the starting point and given the Find command. While ranging at least 50 feet from the handler, the dog searches for the victim. Once the dog has found the victim, he should give the Alert as trained. If it is a Re-find Alert, the dog should return to the handler to give his Alert. If it is a Bark Alert and the dog stays with the victim, the dog should bark continuously until the handler arrives.

In a natural Alert, the handler should know exactly when the dog has found the victim. Because of liability, it is not a good idea to depend only on the natural Alert. It is best to use a visible or audible Alert that anyone can recognize.

LEVEL 2: ADVANCED RE-FIND

There are two schools of thought about this phase of SAR work. One teaches the dog that the entire operation is not over until he brings the handler in to the victim. The other concept is that the exercise is over when the dog returns to the handler after finding the victim. The dog is given the Find command over and over until the handler and dog are next to the victim. In other words, there is no new command, but merely a repeat of the Find exercise. The dog returns, gives his Alert and does it all over again.

GOAL: To teach the dog that you do not always see the victim and that the dog must lead you in to the victim.

OBJECTIVE: To help the dog learn he must get you next to the victim.

METHOD

Once the dog consistently returns to you and gives a reliable Alert after he has found the victim, the Show-me exercise can begin. Set up the problem in the same manner as the Re-find. Initially, the area should encompass about 50 to 100 feet so the steps of the exercise can be done quickly. This communicates to the dog that he must get you to the victim. The victim is to ignore the dog when the dog finds him. As soon as the dog finds his victim and returns to you, immediately giving his Alert, give him the Find command. Tell the dog Show-me as you and the dog run to the victim.

The dog may have to be led back to the victim a number of times for him to get the idea. When the dog comes back to the handler and gives the Alert, do not praise. Rather, give the Show-me command so he leads you immediately to the victim. As soon as the dog reaches the victim, he should get his reward and be praised by the handler and the victim.

PROBLEMS

The dog may get the idea the exercise is finished when he either finds the victim or comes back to his handler. If this happens, withhold all praise until the dog leads you back in to the victim. Teaching the dog the Go To exercise can help clarify the Show-Me concept for the dog.

If the dog does not perform acceptably, return to the previous level of training.

Chapter 9
Advanced Levels of SAR Training

Advanced levels of training are used to practice search techniques, perfect dog/handler skills, and test ability. This stage polishes what the dog has learned up to this point. The dog must have mastered all his search skills by this level. If you or your dog begin to have problems with search techniques, return to previous levels for retraining.

At advanced levels of training, you can hide victims in small debris piles; often on a wilderness search you will encounter debris or junk piles that must be searched. Introducing debris piles also prepares your dog for different types of disaster training.

Be sure to assess each problem and allow the dog to have whatever rest and water breaks he needs. However, it is not a good idea to feed your dog during a problem or to allow the dog to drink too much water. This is especially important for breeds prone to torsion and bloat. Check with your veterinarian about your dog and his risk of torsion and bloat in a working situation.

General Rules for Working All Area Problems

When you are given the boundaries of your problem, review them on the topographical map. Familiarize yourself with all terrain features. Figure out which direction the wind is blowing and position yourself at the point on the edge of your sector which gives the dog the best advantage the wind and terrain will allow. This may be in the corner of the sector or in the middle of one boundary of the sector. How wide you grid and where you work depends on how far your dog will range, the density of the brush, the weather conditions, terrain, and availability of the wind. Each problem is unique; it requires you to analyze the conditions each time you work.

Generally, you work tighter grids in dense brush or woods because the scent has more chance to be trapped. An area that is relatively open with a steady breeze can be worked with wider grids. The width of your grid is determined by the distance your dog will range.

In rocky and hilly terrain with many features that can channel scent, you may want the dog to work closer to be sure that he investigates all the terrain features. A dog who is young and fresh will tend to overshoot or pass by areas where the scent can pool. A slower, more experienced dog will know to check out these areas and search methodically.

In dry, hot, still conditions or in conditions in which you must work in tall grass, weeds or dense vegetation, you need the dog to work close to you. The scent tends to rise straight up from the source, and it is easy for the dog to miss the scent unless he nearly walks over the source.

See the illustrations.

LEVEL 1: TRAIL PROBLEMS

GOAL: To test the dog's search skills and to begin conditioning the dog for area problems.

OBJECTIVE: To have the dog find a person in a short, wilderness/trail setting.

METHOD:

The dog must master the Find, Alert, and Re-find before he begins this level. In a wooded or brushy area approximately one-half mile long, along a dirt trail, road, or access way, place the victim no more than 20 feet off the trail. Do not allow the victim to walk along the trail when going to hide he should approach from a different direction. For the first couple of exercises, know both your victim's location and exactly when the dog finds the victim. Pay close attention to your dog so you can learn the little mannerisms of how your dog works. A dog may get excited when he picks up a scent and "dance," or he might flag his tail a certain way, etc. Each dog develops individual characteristics of his Alert—some less detectable than others. It is important to read these characteristics. This is also a good time to correct any bad habits the dog may be developing before they become unmanageable.

Once the victim is in place, send the dog out to find. The dog must range 50 feet or more, show enthusiasm, demonstrate he is working, and be under control. He must find the victim, give an Alert, and do a Re-find as required by the method used.

PROBLEMS:

At this point in the training, if all of the previous levels have been mastered, there should be no major problems with the search skills. However, different problems may occur, such as game chasing. Dogs may begin to run off at this level because of their enthusiasm or their feelings of greater freedom. If this occurs, correct it immediately. If the dog fails in any aspect of search work or obedience, go back to the level before the problem exercise and retrain.

TEST:

Set the test on a dirt road or trail through light brush or woods about one-half-mile long and 20 feet on either side of the trail. Hide the victim at least 60 yards upwind from the starting point. Once the victim is hidden, the handler decides the starting point in his area and explains the reason he wants to start at this point. The handler is not told where the victim is hidden; he must clear the area (either find the victim or determine that the victim is not in the area) using the method best suited for the problem. The dog should show a strong desire to work and not hesitate when sent out on the Find command. The dog should range at least 50 feet from the handler and take directional commands in order for the handler to keep the dog within the area of the problem. When the dog finds the victim, he should give the Alert as he was trained to do and do a Re-find if it is required.

LEVEL 2: BEGINNING AREA PROBLEM

GOAL: To heighten the dog's anticipation and endurance for wilderness searching.

OBJECTIVE: The dog learns to search a larger area and gains experience maneuvering search obstacles.

METHOD:

This level may take a while for the dog to attain. Training for this level should not be started until the dog has mastered his Level 1 Trail Find, Alert, and Re-find skills. Level 2 training should start on an acre and work up to cover about 10 acres. At times, you need to know the location of your victim to understand the reason the dog is working the way he is. At other times, test to see if you and the dog can work through the problem without knowing where the victim is hidden. This exercise is the heart of wilderness search work.

It is still important at this point to know when your dog finds the victim. This means that both the victim and the handler must have a radio so the victim can tell the handler exactly when the dog finds him and what the dog does. The handler can also let the victim know that the dog has returned and given his Alert and that he is on the way back. At times, the handler will want to change the victim's instructions to enhance the problem for the dog.

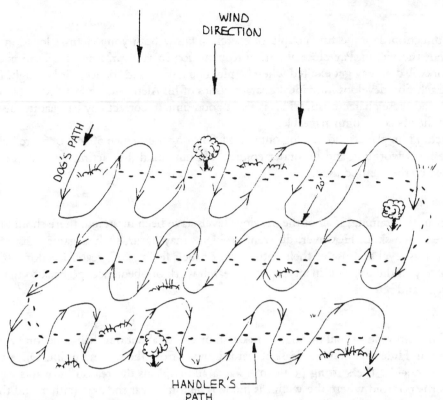

WIND
DIRECTION

DOG'S PATH

HANDLER'S
PATH

Canine team grid pattern, a zigzag grid to work the wind. Drawing by Joseph T. McNichol.

Set up the problem with the victim at least 100 yards away. The dog should find the victim, give his Alert, and do a Re-find. As the dog performs satisfactorily, increase the distance and difficulty of the exercise until you can work a problem that takes an hour to solve. It is important for the dog to have a "Find" each time you train and to alternate shorter problems with longer problems—this is what you will encounter on a real search. You want to be certain the dog will work through thick brush, open fields, water, and hilly as well as flat terrain. Be sure to include in training all of the terrain features you are likely to encounter on a real search.

Work the dog until he just starts to show disinterest or tiring. Keep increasing the distance gradually, until the dog will work when he is tired—but be careful not to work the dog to exhaustion. The dog must Find, Alert, and Re-find when he is tired. Keep in mind that dogs one year and under tire more quickly than dogs in their prime. Young dogs tend to work faster, which tires them sooner. Also, be careful not to push the mature, out-of-shape dog. Dogs need to be conditioned gradually, just as people do.

PROBLEMS:

At the beginning of Level 2, you may believe the dog is working inconsistently. You are not yet aware of the true conditions under which the dog must work; in reality, the dog is doing the best job he can with the scent available. Before you fault the dog for not working, try to assess the wind, weather, and other conditions that affect the scent.

If you rule out scent availability as the problem, you must figure out why your dog is not working well. Go back to the level at which the dog worked well consistently; retrain from there. Check your log book to review the previous exercises to determine if certain weather conditions bother your dog. Pushing a dog too fast is another common mistake, especially with young dogs. Let the dog work at his own pace. Remember, as the size of the area the dog is required to work increases, the dog's stamina and concentration must increase as well. This demands motivation and conditioning. If the dog is not motivated to continue working, he will not do the job he has to do.

As the time of the problem lengthens and the dog becomes increasingly tired, pay close attention to the dog to decide if he is still working and not just walking around. Sometimes it may be difficult to tell when the dog stops working. You may only know when the dog either finds his victim or passes his victim by. When working obstacles with a tired dog, keep in mind that his distance and depth perception are not as good as a human's. Be careful!

TEST:

Set this test in any weather, any terrain, in an area no less than 10 acres. The victim is hidden in an area unknown to the handler. The handler outlines his search strategy at the beginning of the problem according to the terrain, weather, and other conditions. The tester sets a time limit for the problem based on the type of terrain to be searched. The dog must perform a reliable Find, Alert, and Re-find. Never break radio silence to help the handler locate the victim's position. The tester evaluates search techniques, including field safety, the dog's drive and continued desire to work, as well as the actual mechanics of the Search and Find.

LEVEL 3: ADVANCED AREA PROBLEM

GOAL: To bring the dog to wilderness search readiness.

OBJECTIVE: To increase the dog's stamina and level of performance, and to solidify the handler's ability to read his dog.

METHOD:

Once the dog can work approximately 10 acres with no problem, it is time to expand the search area. Now is the time to work consistently on problems in which you do not know where the victim is hidden. A handler can unconsciously signal his dog when he sees the victim first, and the dog can learn to look for these signals rather than do the work himself. When you do not know the location of the victim and cannot possibly see the victim before the dog, you must rely on the dog alone to find the victim. This system builds handler/dog teamwork and develops your trust in your dog. A very hard lesson to learn.

Work this exercise as three separate problems. In the first problem, a lone victim is hidden. The second problem has more than one victim in the area (no more than three). Each victim should be placed in a different location in the search sector. A third problem has no victim in the area. This is the situation you will most often encounter on a real search. It helps to have someone set up the problem for you so you will not know how many, if any, victims are hidden in the designated search area. However, you should be told the maximum number of victims. The problem is usually set up by the head trainer of a unit or someone assigned to the task. The search area can be up to one square mile, 640 acres in flat or gently rolling terrain, which should take about eight hours to complete. In this level of training, you perfect your ability to read your dog's Alert and interpret the meaning of his response to scent. You also practice your clue awareness skills based on the dog's Alerts. After the no-victim-in-the-area problem, another short problem should be set up for the dog so he can have a quick Find. The dog should never leave search training without finding a victim. On a real search, if the dog does not find the victim, a good dog handler will arrange a Find for his dog as soon after the search as possible.

PROBLEMS:

This level of training is a real test of the dog's previous training, and it is not unusual for dogs to fail at this time. A dog may fail because the dog has really been following your lead and not making the Finds hidden. New handlers often give into this temptation because they are afraid their dogs will fail. Consequently, when you do not know the location of the victim, the dog will fail because he has been taught to read your signals.

There are other reasons that a handler loses confidence in the dog's ability to do the work. It is at this stage of training that you learn to trust your dog. Typically, you decide the victim is in one place, or judge that the victim could not be in a particular place because "no one would go there." Then, when the dog correctly indicates the site, you walk away. Now the dog must decide to be either obedient and follow you away from the victim or perform "obedient disobedience" and insist you go in to the victim. If you have not paid close enough attention to your dog, you will lack confidence in your dog's Alerts.

If you are insecure and cannot work at this level, or if the dog has failed for any reason, return to the previous level. Focus on the aspect of training that is giving the dog and/or you a problem.

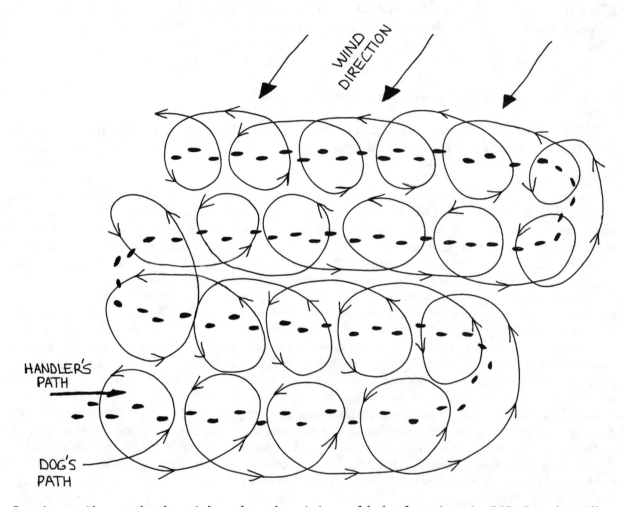

Learning to grid an area based on wind, weather and terrain is one of the key factors in canine SAR. Some dogs will zigzag across your direction of travel while others form a circular pattern. This is called ranging. The object is that your dog searches the area around you for scent. Drawing by Joseph T. McNichol.

TEST:

Test 1: Set the test in any weather conditions. The area should be one-quarter square mile (160 acres) to one square mile (640 acres) in size. One victim is placed by an assistant so that the handler does not know the location until the dog has a Find.

The handler defines his search area clearly on a topographical map, identifying his starting point as well as any clues he or his dog find. He plans his search strategy according to the terrain and weather conditions. This problem should not take more than eight hours for 640 acres in moderate terrain. The dog continues to work even when he is tired.

Test 2. The same conditions as in Test 1 but with two or three victims hidden. The handler is told how many victims are hidden in the area. The victims should not be placed next to each other.

Test 3. The same conditions as in Test 1, but without any victims hidden in the area. The handler is not told there are no victims but is told he has zero to three victims hidden. A clue can be left in the area, such as a piece of clothing or an object. It should be obvious to the handler that the object is not litter or irrelevant debris.

LEVEL 4: BEGINNING NIGHT PROBLEM

GOAL: To develop night searching skills for both you and the dog.

OBJECTIVE: To make the dog aware of the fact that you cannot see well at night.

METHOD:

Start with an area of about five acres that is safe to walk in at night—relatively flat with no holes, cliffs, ledges, mine shafts, etc. The area should include light brush, trees, and paths. The victim is placed about midway in the area close to a path. It helps if some light is attached to the dog's SAR coat or collar. A headlamp, flashlight, or chemical light stick can be used. Be sure it is safe and will not catch on anything or cause the dog injury. You should also use a flashlight and a helmet light.

For safety reasons, the victim must be able to contact either the handler or the base by way of hand-held radios. As you work through the woods, encourage the dog to work close to you by calling him back frequently and by encouraging the dog to work slower. It is amazing how many dogs naturally work close, seeming to understand that people cannot see well in the dark. Night searching is one reason a dog must give a very readable Alert. Often, you will not see the dog until he is right in front of you. Night searching requires the dog to lead you right in to the victim or give a good Bark Alert.

PROBLEM:

Your dog may not lead you close enough to the victim for you to see where the victim is hiding. To correct this, encourage the dog to lead you close enough to the victim to touch him. Withhold the dog's reward until you and dog are right next to the victim and can touch him.

TEST:

Test in fair weather, after dark. The area should be five to ten acres that are safe to walk through. Place one victim in the area. The handler decides which equipment to use, such as a light stick for the dog attached to his reflective vest, a flashlight, and a helmet light, plus the standard daytime equipment required by the unit. The handler outlines the most effective search strategy for the conditions. The dog must work close to the handler. The dog provides a readable or audible Alert and brings his handler right in to the victim.

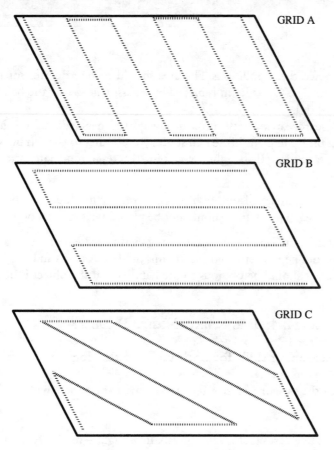

GRID A

GRID B

GRID C

The starting point used to grid a sector will depend upon the wind, terrain and weather. Always start in a location that gives your dog the best advantage. Drawing by Joseph T. McNichol.

LEVEL 5: ADVANCED NIGHT PROBLEM

GOAL: To refine the dog's night searching skills.

OBJECTIVE: To expand the dog's night search area.

METHOD:

    Start this level of the night search problem in the same way as Level 4. Expand the area until you can search up to 40 acres. Never night search areas that are dangerous. Always be aware of roads and traffic. When you can handle 40 acres without knowing where your victim is hidden, consider yourself proficient in night searching.

PROBLEMS:

    While most dogs seem to be aware that the handler cannot see as well at night, some do not catch on and range much too far for the handler to keep sight of them. In such instances, the dog could head off in one direction and the handler in another.

    Theoretically, the dog should communicate to the handler when he finds a scent but, despite a reliable Alert, most handlers like to know for sure where the dog is working. At night, this requires the dog to work closer than during the day. A dog who ranges too far can be corrected by stopping frequently and waiting for the dog to return to you. This gets the dog in the habit of checking to see where you are and encourages the dog to stay closer.

Many handlers use light sticks on their dogs, a good practice. Some handlers use a bell on their dogs so they can hear where the dog is working. This is not always a good idea because the dog can be upset by the constant ringing near his ears. The noise can also interfere with the dog's ability to hear the faint sounds that the victim sometimes makes. A bell is not reliable in conditions in which other noise can prevent you from hearing it.

TEST:
The same as the Level 4 Test with the area expanded to 40 acres.

LEVEL 6: HEAVY BRUSH PROBLEM

GOAL: To expose the dog to heavy brush situations.

OBJECTIVE: To teach the dog to work a heavy brush area in a set time limit.

METHOD:
Work an area of heavy brush cover with one hidden victim. You are unaware of the victim's location. Give the dog the Find command. He should work the area as needed to find the victim. This problem should not be attempted until the dog has perfected his search skills and stamina level.

PROBLEMS:

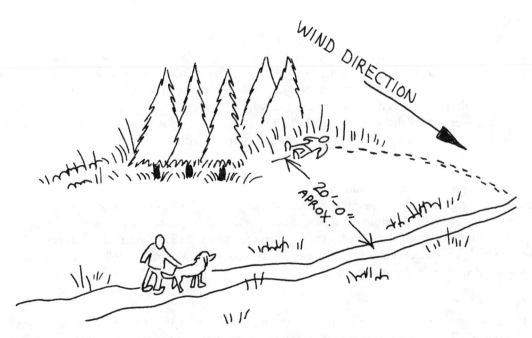

Trail Problem: The victim is hidden approximately 20 feet on either side of a trail within one-half mile distance. Drawing by Joseph T. McNichol.

Certain areas of the country have brush with broad leaves, such as mountain laurel, which tends to trap the scent given off by the victim. Very little, if any, of the scent escapes the dense brush. It is important to get the dog accustomed to searching through this type of brush. Some dogs want to go around thick brushy areas rather than go through them. In certain weather (hot, still days, for example), the scent will not escape from dense brush and the dog must work through each patch of brush to find the victim. During training, expose the dog to dense groundcover so you and the dog will learn how to handle this terrain. If the dog is reluctant to go into thick brush, either point to the area and give him the command to go in or lead the dog in to encourage him. Take extreme care when working through thick brush, especially brush that has thorns, so the dog is not injured. Gradually, the dog will learn how to handle thick brush to avoid getting hurt. No matter how much you train, you will sometimes encounter situations in which the dog can't get into the brush. In those cases, the dog must work around these locations that include brush, tree falls and swamps, to clear the area and look for scent.

TEST:

Test in any weather conditions, a 10-to-40-acre area that has a substantial amount of heavy brush. The dog/handler team must search the area thoroughly. If the dog cannot go through the brush or into it, he must be willing to work around the brush to clear the area.

LEVEL 7: MULTIPLE VICTIM PROBLEM

GOAL: To reinforce the concept for the dog that there can be more than one victim in the area.

OBJECTIVE: To teach that, on a single mission, the dog must find and indicate more than one victim.

METHOD:

Once the dog has mastered all previous levels, you are ready for the acid test of wilderness search. Because a multiple-victim search is not unusual, practice a multiple-victim problem. An assistant places two to four victims in an area at least one-quarter mile square, about 160 acres. When the dog finds one victim, praise him for it and then give the command to Find again. Continue to search the area until you are sure you have covered it thoroughly. When you are finished, your assistant will let you know if you have found all the victims. It is important for the victim's safety that the assistant knows who the victims are, how many there are, and where they are hidden. He must maintain radio contact with them.

PROBLEMS:

Sometimes the dog will consider the training over after he has found the first victim. If this happens, psych the dog up in the same manner you did at first and give him the Find command. Some dogs will go back to the first victim and "find" him over again. If the dog does this, praise the dog and encourage him with a very enthusiastic Find command, pointing away from the victim. As soon as the dog leaves the first victim to continue to look, encourage him on. The found victim should return to base or follow behind the dog/handler team instead of waiting in the woods alone.

TEST:

Place two to four victims, hidden by an assistant, in an area of any terrain and weather conditions and about 160 acres. The victims can be placed in any spatial relationship to one another. The dog/handler team must find the victims within a specified amount of time (appropriate for the terrain). Ideally, the problem should not take more than five hours. If the team misses a victim or two, the team can return to the area to look again.

LEVEL 8: BEGINNING MOVING VICTIM PROBLEM

PURPOSE:

Often in a search situation, the victim will be moving throughout the area. During one actual search, several search teams were coming and going out of base, and the victim wandered into the base camp and mingled with the searchers undetected. More often, the victim is confused, in a state of shock or just trying to find his way out. This is why it is important for the dog to learn to Alert on a moving victim. At times, the dog will Alert on other searchers he encounters; that is okay. The handler must follow up on every Alert to determine if it is viable.

NOTE: For all moving victim problems and tests, be certain the distance between the handler and victim is great enough to allow the victim time to get up and move to another spot before the dog returns to the victim on the Re-find. Be sure to mix the moving victim problems with stationary victim problems or the dog may become reluctant to do Re-finds for fear the victim may not be where he left him.

GOAL: To teach the dog the victim may not be where he left him.

OBJECTIVE: To have the dog find a victim who has moved.

METHOD:

Instruct a victim to go into an area that is a mixture of brush, woods, and open areas, including trails. Have the victim avoid the trails and walk through the brush and woods. It is okay if the victim goes through open areas as well, but the victim should not hide in an open area. In other words, place the victim where the dog expects to find his victims. The difference is that the victim changes location.

As soon as the dog finds the victim and returns to you, the victim moves to a new location a few hundred feet away, upwind. When the dog returns to you and gives the Alert, respond with praise in the usual manner. When you and the dog return to the location where the victim was hidden and the victim is gone, encourage the dog to find the victim (if the dog does not look on his own). In this problem, the dog who is cross-trained to airscent and track/trail is at an advantage. The dog can be told to follow the track of the victim. In some cases, he will do this naturally.

PROBLEMS:

The dog may give up after he returns on the Re-find and the victim is gone. If this happens, get excited and give the dog the Find or Show-me command and encourage the dog to follow in the direction the victim traveled. If this method fails, lead the dog to the victim. Then, repeat the problem from the beginning. This time, when the victim moves, have him hide close to the first hiding place, anticipating that the dog will have no problem finding the victim the second time. Be sure to give the dog a lot of praise when he finds the victim the second time. As the dog gets the idea, increase the distance between the first and second hiding places.

TEST:

Set the test conditions in any weather, any terrain, in an area large enough to allow some distance between the victim and handler. The victim is hidden in the usual manner and the dog sent out. When the dog returns to the handler, the victim moves a few hundred feet away, upwind. The dog returns on a Re-find and leads the handler to the victim in his new hiding place.

LEVEL 9: INTERMEDIATE MOVING VICTIM PROBLEM

GOAL: To teach the dog that the victim can be walking.

OBJECTIVE: To have the dog find a victim who is walking, then return, give an Alert, and either lead you back to the walking victim or stay with the victim and bark.

METHOD:

Set up the problem as in Level 8. When the dog reaches the victim on the Re-find, have the victim get up from his second hiding place and start to walk away very slowly. Keep a little further behind the dog than usual so he has ample time to work out the problem. The dog should go back to you and lead you to the victim. If the dog seems confused, point to the walking victim and give the dog the Find command, walking behind the dog and toward the victim. If you want the dog to give a Bark Alert and stay with the victim, have the victim stop as soon as the dog barks. By stopping when the dog barks, the victim will be passively rewarding the dog for barking.

PROBLEM:

The dog may not want to lead you to the walking victim; he may be confused about whether the person is indeed the victim. If the dog hesitates or looks confused, get excited, point to the victim and give the dog the Find command. Join the dog and point to the victim, who is still walking slowly. Encourage the dog to advance to the victim as you command, Find. Avoid leading the dog. You want to communicate to the dog that he is to lead.

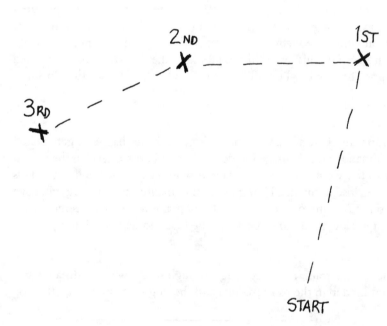

Multiple Victim Problem: In some situations there may be more than one person lost. Your dog should be able to find more than one person in an area. Drawing by Joseph T. McNichol.

TEST:
This test is set in any weather conditions. The victim is hidden in the usual manner with enough distance to allow him enough time to move after the dog has found him. When the dog leaves the victim to alert the handler, the victim exits his hiding place and, if the dog is doing a Re-find, starts to walk slowly away. The dog should lead the handler to the now moving victim. If the dog is giving a Bark Alert, the victim slowly walks until the dog finds him. When the dog barks, the victim stops and waits for the handler.

LEVEL 10: ADVANCED MOVING VICTIM

GOAL: To have the dog learn that the victim can be moving continuously.

OBJECTIVE: To train the dog to find a victim who is moving, return to you, give an Alert, and lead you back to the victim.

METHOD:
The victim goes into an area and leaves a scent pool by sitting or standing in one spot for a few minutes. Then the victim continues to walk, taking care to mark the direction in which he left the area. Send your dog out for a Find, following as closely as possible. The dog should find the spot where the victim stopped. When the dog reaches the place where the victim rested, he should continue to follow the hot scent in the direction the victim traveled. If the dog does not continue in the right direction, encourage the dog to go that way until he leads you to the victim (who continues to walk away slowly). If the dog has been taught to track, he can be given the Track command when he finds the scent pool and be allowed to track or trail his victim. You then catch up to the victim and greet him in a friendly manner. Both the victim and handler praise the dog.

PROBLEM:
The dog may not understand the walking victim is the person he must find. In some cases, the dog may not give an Alert on the walking victim. This can be a difficult problem for the dog, since in past training other searchers in the party were always walking and the victim was always stationary. The victim should contact you when the dog approaches him. If the dog does not return to you on his own and give an Alert, return to Level 9. If the dog will not approach the victim, the victim should squat down and encourage the dog. The victim can offer the dog a tug toy, ball or treat.

LEVEL 11: MORE ADVANCED MOVING VICTIM

GOAL: To solidify the moving victim Find for the dog.

OBJECTIVE: To have the dog find a moving victim in areas where he is not used to finding a victim.

METHOD:
Set up the problem as in Level 10. The victim walks in open areas and on trails. The victim should not walk in the places where the dog is accustomed to finding a victim. The dog should do a Find, Alert and Re-find, leading you to the moving victim. Once the dog finds his moving victim in all situations, a problem can be set up with two or more people walking together.

If the dog has difficulty with this variation, go back to the previous levels until the dog understands what is expected of him. It is important to communicate to the dog that anyone can be the victim, whether the person is lying down, walking, on trails or in brush. The dog must also learn that there can be more than one victim in a group. This can only be done by setting up problems to simulate real search situations. A good exercise to teach the concept that the victim can be a group of people is to have four to six people sit together quietly and have the dog find the group.

TEST:

The test should be set up the same as for the Level 10 Test. The main difference is that the victim walks in areas where the dog is not used to finding victims, such as trails, open areas, etc. The dog should give an Alert and Re-find or give a Bark Alert.

Chapter 10
The Scent Discriminatory Dog

There are three types of scent discriminatory dogs. The *tracking dog* keeps his nose in the footprints of the person he is looking for; he generally works in a harness, on-leash. The *trailing dog* does not necessarily keep his nose in the footprints, but works a few feet from the person's trail, starting from a scent article. He also works on-leash. The *scent-discriminatory, airscenting dog* works off-leash, airscenting, but Alerts only on the scent of the person he is looking for. All types of scent discrimination training are often called tracking.

Because there are many books written on how to train a tracking dog, we will not cover all of the methods used to teach a dog to follow a specific scent; however, we will highlight the basic principles of scent discriminatory training as it applies to the SAR dog. The basics apply to all three types of scent discriminatory dogs. The handler must decide what type of scent discriminatory dog he wants and train for that specific method.

There are several circumstances that affect a dog's performance. Always give the weather conditions careful consideration. The dynamics of scent are covered in the chapter, "Wind, Scent, and Dog." If your dog does not work well one day but has done well before, discontinue training and wait for more favorable conditions. If you find you reach a certain level and your dog does not respond, go back to the previous level and start over. Your dog is most likely not working because he does not understand what is expected of him.

Until you reach Level 9, all training should be in areas that are relatively uncontaminated, which means no human scent on the article except the person who is the victim. Train in wilderness, woods, or fields. Train in all weather so you can learn how varied conditions affect your dog's ability to work a trail. However, keep in mind that the best time to train a tracking dog is when there is some moisture on the ground in early morning or early evening.

Be sure to consider different theories about scent and the dog's ability to detect scent. Some people claim the dog does not follow the scent of the person at all, but the crushed vegetation where the person walked. They believe the dog can detect the difference in tracks by the degree of pressure or weight of the person who made the track and can tell weight differences among people to within five pounds. Others think the dog follows the scent from flakes of dead skin that decompose due to bacteria. And some believe the dog uses a combination of different scents.

Some maintain that a dog can track on hard surfaces through city streets, and indeed, many dogs do. Others contend that the dog cannot work near a highway because the fumes from cars destroy the dog's ability to detect the scent. Most trainers agree that a dog left where he breathes exhaust fumes for any length of time, such as the cargo area of an airplane or the back of a poorly ventilated pickup truck, temporarily loses his ability to detect scent.

Keep in mind that all dogs are different and no one breed is best for scent work. Some individual dogs can work in environments where others cannot, and some breeds may do best with certain types of scent work. However, performance depends upon the ability of the individual dog. If the dog loves the work, he will give you his best. Training to track is fundamental in preparing a dog for SAR.

LEVEL 1: RUNAWAY

NOTE: For scent discrimination training, the scent article is important. It is the item used to let the dog know what to find. Try different sorts of scent articles to get the dog used to working from different materials. Initially, scent articles should be made of cloth (the kind is not important) so that the article can hold a strong scent. Later, the dog should be taught to scent off objects made of metal, wood, plastic and many other materials. For all basic training, the scent article should be as "clean" as possible. The article carries only the scent of the victim. For the first few levels of training, this is very important; you are teaching the dog the concept that he has to follow a specific scent.

GOAL: To teach the dog the command to find his human victim.

OBJECTIVE: To have the dog follow his owner, and then an assistant to a hiding place.

METHOD:

See Chapter 7. Level 1: Runaway is the same for scent discriminatory dogs as it is for airscenting dogs. Follow Level 1: Beginning Runaway and Level 2: Intermediate Runaway.

Level 2: Scent Article-Runaway

GOAL: To train the dog to connect the scent article with the victim.

OBJECTIVE: To have the dog smell a scent article and follow the scent to the victim.

METHOD:

Before you attempt to teach the dog about the scent article, the dog must understand that the Find command means to find a victim. The victim holds an uncontaminated scent article toward the dog and drops it as the dog watches. While the dog is still watching, the victim hides within 50 feet of the dog. Take the dog to the scent article and give the dog the command to scent the article, then give the dog the command to find the victim. Scent articles must not be handled by anyone but the victim, or you undo all that you are trying to teach the dog.

A couple of tips might be helpful. Do not give the dog more than one Find command, which is given at the scent article. The reason is simple. It is easy for a green dog to come across another scent while following the original scent. If you give another Find command, the dog can become confused about which scent you want him to look for.

Also, do not allow the dog's head to go down to the ground until you reach the scent article. Then, if you cannot easily get the dog's head down next to the article, drop the dog into a down position with his nose next to the scent article.

Remember, do not touch the scent article yourself. Do not allow other odors to contaminate the scent article, either. This includes the odor of the container the article was stored in. It is best to have the victim store the scent article against his chest, under his shirt, until it is time to place the scent article.

Repeat this exercise until the dog finds his victim without hesitation. Give the dog a strong reward for finding the victim. You may use food; however, food should be discontinued after the dog shows consistent enthusiasm and then only used occasionally to reinforce the training. It is best to train before feeding the dog. Be sure to stay in this phase of the training until the dog associates the scent article with the trail and the victim.

TEST: Level 2

Leave a scent article on the ground at the start of a track. Take the dog to the scent article, show him the scent article and give the command to find the person. The way the dog advances indicates that he knows he is looking for the person connected with the scent article. The dog follows the track until he finds the person at the end of the trail.

LEVEL 3: IDENTIFICATION

GOAL: To have the dog give an Alert to indicate the victim belongs to the scent article.

OBJECTIVE: To give a good found-victim Alert, letting you know the dog has located the person whose scent he was trailing.

METHOD:

This technique is very useful to associate a person with an article and to enable you to know which person the dog has followed in the event the victim is in a group of people.

There are several theories about how to get a dog to identify the victim. One is to have the victim always give the dog a food reward. Once the dog is used to getting a food reward, hide food on the victim. He will go to the victim in search of the food and look for it when he finds the victim. This will encourage the dog to sniff and search the victim.

If you decide not to use the food reward, develop another means for the dog to identify the victim when found. Some handlers look for the dog's natural Alert. If you decide to use the dog's natural Alert, reinforce this behavior so it becomes reliable.

Rather than a natural Alert, you can use the Bark Alert or whatever you feel comfortable with. Decide on a behavior, teach it to the dog, and use it only when he finds his victim. The dog must learn his Alert before he trains in tracking. For a Bark Alert, the dog should be able to speak on command. Then, when the dog finds his victim, he is encouraged to speak.

TEST: Level 3

Set the test on a trail long enough to make the problem a challenge for the dog. The handler explains to the tester what the identifying Alert will be. Take the dog to the beginning of the trail and show him the scent article. Given the Find command, the dog leads the handler directly to the victim. When the dog finds the victim, he gives his Alert, clearly indicating that this specific person is the victim.

LEVEL 4: TOUGHER TRAIL PROBLEM

GOAL: To have the dog follow a trail when he does not see the victim leave.

OBJECTIVE: To identify the scent without seeing the victim lay the trail or leave.

METHOD:

Keep the dog away from the area. Have the victim drop the scent article at the beginning of the trail and lay a trail. At this point, the length of the trail is not important; however, the trail should be long enough to keep the dog's interest. When the victim is hidden, bring the dog to the scent article and give him the Find command. Have the dog give the Alert when he finds his victim. Work on this exercise until the dog is reliable.

At this stage of training, the dog should be brought to the scent article from various directions so he does not think all trails start straight ahead. Encourage the dog to circle the scent article to find the trail by bringing him in at a different angle each time.

Bel Malinwa "Asta" and K. George during tracking drill in park area. Photo by SARDA.

Bloodhound on trail. Andy Rebmann's Clem, working for the CT State Troopers.
Andy and Clem have more than 100 finds. Photo courtesy of Marcia Koenig.

TEST: Level 4

    The victim lays a trail, leaving a scent article at the beginning, then hides. The dog does not see the victim laying the trail and is brought to the trail from a side angle. The dog is shown the scent article, and given the Find command. The dog follows the trail, finds the victim and gives his Alert. The dog either directly follows the trail or casts around to find the trail. He must indicate that he knows what he is looking for.

LEVEL 5: NO SCENT ARTICLE

GOAL: To teach the dog to pick up a track without a scent article.

OBJECTIVE: To train the dog to scent from a foot print.

METHOD:

    The victim lays a trail as in Level 4, but scuffs up the dirt instead of leaving a scent article. Clearly mark the beginning of the trail. A piece of surveyor's tape on a bush or tree is helpful; however, take care that the dog does not pick up on the marker as a scent article.

TEST: Level 5

    The victim lays a trail without leaving a scent article for the dog. The dog and handler do not watch the victim lay the trail. Take the dog to the area, shown him the spot on the ground where the trail begins, and allow him to cast around if he needs to pick up the trail. The dog proceeds directly along the trail until he finds the victim. The dog then gives his Alert.

LEVEL 6: AGED TRAIL

    NOTE: A track or trail that is about one to one-and-a-half hours old will have a great deal of spill-over scent in the area of the laid track. It may cause the dog to trail or airscent instead of track.

GOAL: To enhance the dog's trailing skills.

OBJECTIVE: To trail a victim on an aged and lengthened trail.

METHOD:

    Lay a trail with or without a scent article. It is a good idea to vary the techniques. Age the trail and increase the length. Age the trail in brief increments and increase the length of the trail in increments until you reach one mile in length and 12 hours old. If the dog has difficulty, go back to the previous age and length. It is also a good idea to alternate. In other words, start with a trail that is fresh but lengthened. Next work the same distance with the trail aged until you reach the desired age and length.

TEST: Level 6

    The victim lays a trail, with or without a scent article, three-quarters to one mile long and 10 to 12 hours old. Do not stage this problem during the heat of a summer day. Therefore, during the summer prepare the trail the night before and put the dog on the trail the first thing in the morning, 10 to 12 hours later. Before starting the problem, transport the victim to the end of the trail so he is there when the dog arrives. The victim should not cross the trail he laid earlier. Transport by vehicle if possible. Or, have the victim return to the end of the trail from the opposite direction from the aged trail. The dog is shown the beginning of the trail and is allowed to cast at will. When the dog locates the trail, he follows it enthusiastically to the end where he alerts on the victim.

LEVEL 7: MORE COMPLICATED TRAILS

GOAL: To have the dog learn that trails are not always simple.

OBJECTIVE: To train the dog to find the victim despite complications in the trail.

METHOD:

Create a trail of the age and length attained thus far. Do not increase either element, but have the victim add loops, turns, and some backtracking in the trail. Gradually increase the level of difficulty by having the victim jump over objects to break the trail, walk through water, etc. Also, teach the dog that the victim can be up off the ground by ending the trail with the victim in a tree.

At first, the victim marks his trail when he makes turns, loops, backtracks, etc. This allows you to see how your dog handles the change from the basic, straight trail. As soon as the dog can consistently work through these deviations, the victim stops marking them. When you start varying the trail, give the dog time to work out the problem. Do not interfere, as this causes the dog to depend on you to solve the problem. On real searches, you depend on the dog to lead you.

PROBLEMS:

Often when turns and difficulties are introduced, the dog will overshoot the trail. Let him go when he does; give him a chance to work out the problem. If he loses the trail, bring him back to the point where he lost it and let him start over. After awhile, the dog will learn to circle to find the trail.

TEST: Level 7

The victim lays a trail up to one mile long and 12 hours old. If the victim does not leave a scent article, then he marks the beginning of the trail. The trail includes at least six obstacles, including backtracking, loops, objects and breaks in the trail. The victim returns to the end of the trail without going near or crossing the aged trail. Take the dog to the start of the trail, give the Find command and allow him to work the problem out. When he finds his victim, he gives his Alert.

LEVEL 8: CONTAMINATED TRAIL

GOAL: To have the dog distinguish between two scents.

OBJECTIVE: To train the dog to follow one specific scent out of two, and Alert on the victim.

METHOD:

The victim leaves a scent article at the beginning of the trail and lays a trail of reasonable length. Another person from a different family crosses the trail of the victim. The second person marks the trail where he crossed it. The victim waits at one point in the trail for the other person to intersect it and meet him. When the trail is finished, send the dog out and watch carefully how he reacts when he encounters the second scent. If the dog tries to follow the wrong scent, let him go for a short distance to be sure the scent of the victim has not blown onto the other trail. If it becomes apparent that the dog is following the wrong scent, go back to the intersection, move a little above it, and put the dog on the correct trail.

The Scent Discriminatory Dog, Scent Article Runaway. The victim drops a scent article for the dog to see, then runs away and hides. Drawing by Joseph T. McNichol.

Once the dog can handle simple contamination, use a number of people to contaminate the trail. Vary the ages of the victim's trail and the contaminating trails, so the contaminating trails are newer or fresher than the victim's trail. Eventually, two or three people lay trails side-by-side and the dog follows the victim's trail, identified by a scent article. At one point, the victim should deviate from near the other trails. When the dog can successfully follow a contaminated trail, allow him to track in areas such as school yards and playgrounds that have not been used heavily for a few hours (for example, in late evening). The victim lays a track through these areas and continues to a less contaminated area, so that the track is first difficult and then easy.

TEST: Level 8

Involve three people in laying a trail for the dog. The victim leaves the scent article. The other two travel along the trail left by the victim for about one-quarter and one-half the distance, and then leave the victim's trail. One of the contaminating people leaves a trail older than the victim's and the other should be fresher. Mark the trail clearly so the handler knows if the dog starts to follow the wrong scent. Make the trail long enough to allow the dog to work it out and be interested. Take the dog to the start of the trail, show the scent article, and give the Find command. The dog follows the correct trail, making adjustments as needed if he should stray from the trail. At the end of the trail the dog gives an Alert.

LEVEL 9: AGED TRAIL IN VARIOUS ENVIRONMENTS

GOAL: To give the dog practice in different settings.

OBJECTIVE: To have the dog work comfortably in various settings.

METHOD:
Up to now, you have been working in wooded and less contaminated areas. Now, start working areas such as shopping malls, parking lots, school grounds, livestock yards, railroad tracks, and any other places you think the dog may encounter on a search. Include various indoor flooring, such as carpets, waxed floors, etc. Start with a fresh track through a new area. As the dog follows the trail successfully, age it and lengthen the distance.

TEST: Level 9
Pick a heavily contaminated area, such as a shopping mall or school yard. The presence of people is not necessary, but it should be an area visited by people within a few hours before the exercise. Have the victim

leave a scent article at the beginning of the trail. Lay a trail from one to six hours old and up to one-half mile long through the area. Station the victim at the end of the trail. Bring the dog to the start of the trail and show him the scent article. Give the dog the Find command and allow him to work out the problem. When the dog finds the victim, he should give an Alert.

LEVEL 10: UNKNOWN PERSON

GOAL: To have the dog track someone he does not know.

OBJECTIVE: To teach the dog to track and identify a totally strange scent.

METHOD:

It is likely the victims you have been using have been people the dog knows. Now it is time to arrange for the dog to track a stranger. The victims on a real search will be people the dog does not know. Periodically, over the course of the year, arrange for the dog to track unfamiliar victims. "Victims" can be found in many places: where you work, school, scouts, your place of worship. You may even advertise for volunteers.

Be sure to instruct the victim in exactly what is expected. Have the victim leave a scent article at the beginning of the trail, providing him complete instructions on where to go and on how to mark the trail. Start the dog by showing him the scent article and allowing him to cast if he needs to. The dog should readily follow the trail and find the victim, giving his Alert. The trail should be about one-half mile long and at least one hour old.

TEST: Level 10

The victim is someone the dog has never seen before. The victim leaves a scent article and lays a trail that is at least one-half mile long and one hour old. The victim waits at the end of the trail for the dog. Show the dog the scent article, and allow him to cast for scent. He should follow the trail enthusiastically. When he finds the victim, he gives an Alert.

Casting for a track: The dog should be taken to the scent article and allowed to circle the article if the dog wishes, to look for the trail. Be sure the trail is not always straight ahead from the dog. Drawing by Joseph T. McNichol.

LEVEL 11: ID FROM A GROUP

GOAL: To have the dog identify the victim from a group when given a scent article.

OBJECTIVE: To teach the dog to give a strong indication to match a scent article and person.

METHOD 1

On an actual search, a victim has been known to wander back into base camp and go undetected by the searchers. In other situations, the victim could get mixed up in a group of people. Therefore, practice giving your dog a scent article and have him identify a person who is in a group of people. To do this, have the victim leave a scent article and walk a short distance (about 500 feet) to a group of people. The trail can be straight with no backtracking or other difficulties. Let the dog work out the problem and give you an Alert on the victim. As the dog accomplishes this problem with ease, increase the length and age of the trail.

METHOD 2

Have the victim leave a scent article a few feet from the group or give it to you in a container that is clean and free from human scent. Walk up to the group of people, and focus the dog on the scent article. Have him identify the person from the group without having to follow a trail. It is a good idea to practice with the entire group of people neutral toward the dog as well as friendly to the dog. Be sure the dog does not receive his reward until he makes a clear, readable Alert on the victim. Remember, if at any point the dog has difficulty, go back to the previous level and retrain the dog. Also, consider how weather conditions change the availability of the scent for the dog.

TEST: Level 11

1. Several people (a group of three or more), wait in an area about 500 feet away. These people can be engaged in quiet conversation or merely sitting around, but they should be close together. The victim leaves a scent article, walks 500 feet to the group of people, and joins in their activity. Bring the dog to the beginning of the trail, show him the scent article and give him the Find command. The dog follows the trail, goes up to the victim in the group and gives the Alert.

2. The victim stands in a group of three or more people. The handler walks to the group of people and the victim gives the handler the scent article in an uncontaminated container. The handler walks away from the group and scents the dog on the container, giving the dog the Find command. The dog searches the area until he finds the victim and gives an Alert that identifies the victim. While the dog is walking around the area, some people are neutral toward the dog and others are friendly.

LEVEL 12: CONTAMINATED SCENT ARTICLE

NOTE: Until now you have used an uncontaminated scent article for training. However, in real life, an uncontaminated scent article is not always available. Sometimes you have to collect scent from objects and you have no way of knowing what scent is on the object in addition to that of the missing person. A dog can be trained to work from a contaminated scent article. For those who doubt, consider the following: Probably the uncontaminated scent article you have been using is not really clean. The article has the scent of the material it is made of on it, and also the floating skin cells of the people in the area. If the material is cloth, it contains the scents of the dyes, the fabric, the soap it was washed in, and the dust has it collected from sitting around. In the average household, the dust is 75 percent human skin cells—

so you can understand why it is almost impossible to have a truly uncontaminated scent article. Therefore, you have been teaching your dog to sort out the scents on the object, and by association with the trail left by your victim, learn how to decide which scent to follow. You have also introduced the dog to the concept that he must sort out different human scents when you asked him to follow a contaminated track. The next step in training is to teach the dog to make a finer distinction between scent articles.

GOAL: To have the dog follow the track of a person from a mildly contaminated scent article.

OBJECTIVE: To teach the dog to distinguish which human scent to follow from two different scents.

METHOD:

Use a clean cloth article, such as a bandanna, which has been kept next to the skin of your victim for about one-half hour. Have the victim hand the article to another person, and then leave to lay his track. Have the second person drop the article on the ground and leave in a different direction from the victim. Next, bring the dog into the area, scent him on the article, and allow him to follow the correct track. If he chooses the wrong track, show him the correct track and praise him for following it. When he finds the victim, give him lots of praise.

TEST: Level 12

Using a lightly contaminated scent article and two people, one the victim and one the "other" person, allow the dog to follow a fresh track made by the victim.

PROBLEMS:

If the dog does not follow the correct track after a few tries, have the victim hand the scent article to someone else for a few seconds, and leave, laying a track. Arrange the problem so that the track of the victim is not near the track of the other person. The dog only finds the track of the victim and never comes across the track of the other person.

LEVEL 13: TOUGHER CONTAMINATED SCENT PROBLEM

GOAL: To have the dog choose the correct track in a side-by-side tracking problem.

OBJECTIVE: To teach the dog to follow the correct trail when given two different scents on an article and two tracks.

METHOD:

The victim and an assistant stand in the same area about 10 feet apart. The victim gives his scent article to another person to hold for a minute or so. The scent article is dropped onto the ground and both parties leave, traveling together for about 20 feet, then going in opposite directions. The victim marks the track where he veered off so the handler knows which track is the correct one. When both people are in place, the dog is taken to the scent article and given the command to Find the victim. If the dog has trouble finding the correct trail at the point where they veer off, the handler should restart the dog at the point where the two trails separate.

TEST: Level 13

The victim hands his scent article to the assistant who holds it for a minute or so. They drop the scent article on the ground and both people leave the area, laying a trail for 20 feet or more. After 20 feet, both parties separate, going in opposite directions. The handler waits for about 20 minutes after the victim is hidden and then sends the dog on the track. The dog leads the handler to the victim.

PROBLEMS:

If the dog does not follow the correct trail, restart the dog at the point where both parties separated, praising the dog for following the correct trail. If that does not work, go back to the previous level of training.

Once you have accomplished this level of training, add to it by increasing the time and distance of the track. Also, experiment with various ways of collecting scent from objects. For example, take sterile gauze (a first-aid bandage works well) and place it in the scent article (such as a coat) and then use the gauze as your scent article. Or, wipe the steering wheel of a car for scent, thus collecting sweat and skin oils. Practice the situations you will encounter on an actual mission. Gradually, you will learn to trust your dog and know how to read what he is telling you.

Chapter 11
Water Search Training

Water search training requires more detective work than a land search. You cannot see what is going on under the water. Divers must often search by "feel," and the dog handler must rely on his dog. The scent from the body submerged in water floats upward and moves or is carried with the current. When the scent reaches the surface of the water, the air carries it in the direction the wind is blowing. Scent can also collect on debris, such as a log, in the water. The thermoclines (temperature differences) at different water levels will inhibit the scent. A thermocline can keep the scent from reaching the surface, or the scent can travel along a thermocline for quite a distance before breaking through. You have no way to figure out if this is occurring or not.

There are a few other facts that will help you determine why your dog is giving an Alert. After several days in cold water or a few hours in warm water, human skin will sometimes peel off the drowned victim, referred to as skin slippage. The skin will come off hands, for example, like a glove. As the victim is washed along the waterway, some skin may be ripped off and cling to underwater debris. If the body is trapped, marine life and debris can damage the body, causing skin to shred and wash away. It is possible under the right circumstances for the dog to Alert on this skin.

Initially, when a person drowns, the body sinks to the bottom of the water. Later, depending upon the water temperature and gas formation, the body surfaces. Generally, a body surfaces within two or three days in the summer, but may take weeks or months in the winter. In some bodies of water that stay cold all year, such as the Great Lakes, the body may never surface. When the body is only partly submerged, the scent can be carried in any direction, usually determined by the flow of the water and the direction of the wind. A body in a swampy area with a current flowing into a pond, marsh, etc. causes scent to collect throughout the entire body of water, provoking multiple Alerts.

LEVEL 1: PREPARATION FOR WATER TRAINING

GOAL: To introduce the dog to the boat.

OBJECTIVE: To teach the dog to feel comfortable in a boat, and to get in and out without tipping the boat.

METHOD:
It is a good idea to start with a "V" bottom boat (such as a row boat) on land. Let the dog get into the boat, sit in it, move around in it, and get out again until he feels comfortable. The dive squad assigned to the search provides the boat, but the kinds of craft can vary. Therefore, practice on as many varieties as you can.

Once the dog is comfortable with the boat on land, rock the boat with the dog seated inside. Also, bang on the outside of the boat the way it might bang against the dock.

As soon as the dog tolerates the noisy, moving boat on land, try the same exercises in calm water. Let the dog enter and exit the boat from a dock, where he must jump down into the boat and up to get out. Also, position the boat near the shore where he must jump up into the boat or walk into the boat.

Take the dog for a test run. Operate the motor; the dog should be used to the sound of the motor revving and possibly backfiring. Row, so the dog is exposed to and not afraid of oars. Allow the dog to hang over the side with his front paws, maintaining his balance. Some dogs love to swim so much they want to jump in. It is not a good idea to encourage your dog to do this while in search training or on an actual mission. However, if your dog should jump out of the boat, know how to get him back in. One method is to grab your dog by the tail and scruff of the neck while he is parallel with the boat. A better method is to use a nonrestrictive harness that you can grab to hoist the dog. There are also life vests made for dogs with handles on the back designed to lift a dog from the water into the boat. No matter how you do it, keep the dog's head above water while you pull him up. If you try to pull him up by his collar alone, he will become frightened and feel as though he is slipping down into the water. Remember, because the dog is in the water, he will be buoyant and easy to lift. Trying to get your hand under the dog to lift him out of the water increases your chances of falling out or capsizing the boat. A few practice sessions will make you more comfortable about the possibility of your dog falling over during a search and will give the dog trust in you to get him back into the boat.

It is critical that you do not allow your dog to swim in contaminated water. If the dog should get into contaminated water, immediately wash him with a solution of dish soap and water. Rinse thoroughly. Take care that contaminated water and the agent used to decontaminate the dog do not get into his eyes, nose and mouth.

LEVEL 2: BEGINNING WATER TRAINING

GOAL: To teach the dog that someone can be under the water.

OBJECTIVE: To train the dog to Alert on human scent that has reached the surface of the water.

METHOD:
Your dog must be trained in wilderness, airscenting or tracking before doing water work. Often when searching for someone who has drowned, a scent article from the drowned person is not available. Therefore, most water search work is done by the airscenting dog. A scent discriminatory dog can be used when you have a scent article from the drowned victim.

The main objective of the training is to teach the dog that a victim can be under the water. This is a concept most dogs do not have until they are shown. The work is much easier if you have a diver. When using divers for water-search training, work out all details of the training before the diver goes into the water. To be safe, two divers work in the water with a third or fourth on shore. Establish a signal to tell the divers when to surface; the diver must have a way to let you know when he is in place and ready to work. Use a rope between an assistant on shore and the diver or use underwater radio communications.

The dog must learn how to travel in a boat safely. Drawing by Joseph T. McNichol.

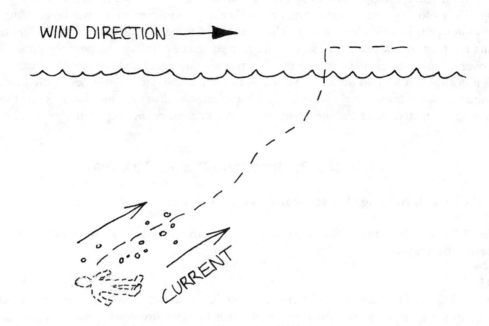

WIND DIRECTION ⟶

CURRENT

The scent rises from the body, is carried with the current until it reaches the surface of the water where the wind will carry it further. Based on the dog's alerts, current, wind and weather, the dog handler must determine an area where the body will most likely be located. This will help the divers find the body. Drawing by Joseph T. McNichol.

Let the dog quietly watch the diver suit up. Once the diver is ready to go into the water, allow the dog to meet the diver. The dog can become frightened or aggressive toward a fully suited diver because he looks and smells differently. Therefore, never force the dog to approach; let the diver entice the dog by calling him. Before the diver enters the water, be sure he has hot dogs (broken in half) to keep under the water as a reward for the dog. When the diver is ready, he wades knee-deep into the water. Bring the dog on-leash to the edge of the water.

As the diver enters the water, encourage the dog as for wilderness runaway training, by saying to the dog in an excited voice, "Where's he going? Where's he going?" When the diver is out of sight, put the dog into the boat. If the shoreline does not permit this, let the dog watch from the boat while the diver sinks into the water. When the diver is in place (determine by waiting for a prearranged time or by a signal from the diver), start working the dog in the boat. Be sure to work downwind and down-current from the diver. If using a gas-powered motor, do not let the gas fumes blow into the dog's face.

Phoenixville Dive Rescue and K-9 unit getting ready to search a river. Photo courtesy of Chief Bob Motzer.

A young dog watching a diver go under the water. The Phoenixville Dive Squad and K-9 Unit. Photo courtesy of Chief Bob Motzer.

Showing a new dog that people can be under the water. The dog is watching the divers go down. Phoenixville Dive Rescue and K-9 Unit. Photo courtesy of Chief Bob Motzer.

Zack, a Golden Retriever, looking for a diver. Photo courtesy of Chief Bob Motzer.

Zack, during water training. Photo courtesy of Chief Bob Motzer.

Water search training by Bruce Speer and Isaac. Photo courtesy of Bob Koenig.

An actual mission. Ness, one of the first Border Collies to be used in SAR, coming out of a boat.

Top: Scout, the first SAR Beauceron in the U.S. Middle: Base camp for search for two missing ice divers. Bottom: Scout, looking for scent.

Top: Scout looking for scent. Middle: Scout has hit on scent. Bottom: Ness verifies the scent.

Give the dog the Find command and zigzag, cutting across the current and wind. As the dog gets excited when he picks up the scent from the diver, encourage him. When you near the diver, signal either by banging on the boat or by pulling a signal line attached to the diver, so he will know it is time to come up. When the diver surfaces, have him give the dog a piece of the hot dog and both handler and diver praise the dog.

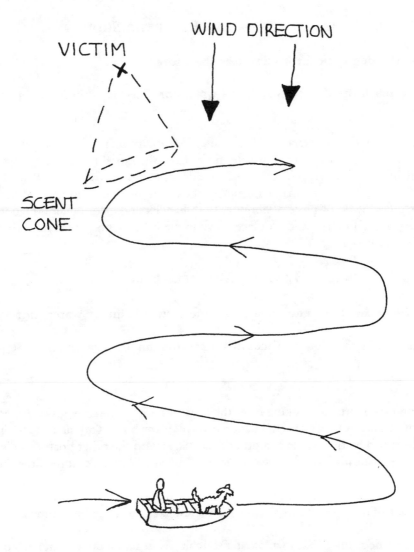

Grid pattern on water: It is important to use the same principles to grid a body of water as you would a section of land. If your boat has a gas motor, be sure the fumes do not flow into the dog's face. Drawing by Joseph T. McNichol.

Remember to start the zigzag pattern far enough down-current and downwind for the dog to find the scent. This is why a still body of water is much better for training dogs than one that is swiftly moving. If the current is strong and fast, the scent will be carried too far before it comes to the surface. It is disappointing when the dog gets excited about finding the scent from the diver and then the diver surfaces far from the dog. However, in still water the dog will see and hear the air bubbles from the diver. You must be careful to avoid teaching the dog to alert on the bubbles alone.

LEVEL 3: WORKING FROM THE SHORE

GOAL: To have the dog look for bodies near the shore.

OBJECTIVE: To teach the dog to search the water for victims while he is on land.

METHOD:

You do not need a diver to practice this exercise. Be careful to ensure the safety of all handlers, assistants, and dogs. In a safe area with graduating water depth from the shore, (no sudden drops) place a victim in the water, partially hidden by weeds, etc., with his shoulders and head above water. Start the dog downwind from the victim and give the Find command. Encourage the dog to work the shoreline. When the dog finds the victim, the victim gives the dog a piece of hot dog. Both handler and victim praise the dog. For variety, the victim may wear a mask and snorkel and float face down in the water, ignoring the dog when found. The dog should do a Re-find, or Bark Alert.

LEVEL 4: MULTIPLE BOATS

GOAL: To reinforce the dog's knowledge that the victim is under water, not above.

OBJECTIVE: To train the dog to focus his attention on the water and not people in other boats.

METHOD:

Once the dog is comfortable working from the boat and has consistently given Alerts to a diver in the water, introduce more boats. Often a search situation involves many boats working close to one another. Commonly, a dog is distracted by the people and other boats. Start with the other boats at a distance so as not to distract the dog; then, gradually have them work closer. When the dog looks at the other boats, give him his Find command and point to the water to redirect his attention. When he looks back to the water and starts to search, praise him. If he persists in focusing his attention on the other boats, tell him No and redirect his attention to the water. If this does not work after a few tries, have the other boats move away until the dog is barely distracted.

It does not take a dog long to learn what water searching is all about, but be careful. You do not want the dog to Alert on garbage; avoid using clothing in place of a live person. It is possible to use "cadaver," body parts or items used to simulate body parts like hair, teeth, finger and toe nails, in place of a diver. However, the best and most efficient work is done with a diver.

Keep in mind that water work is stressful: depending on search conditions, you may need to give a dog frequent rests on shore. Be aware that no matter how hard you may try to stop them, many dogs bite and drink the water; this means they have to relieve themselves more frequently. Periodic shore breaks are necessary.

TEST: Level 4

Submerge a diver in at least eight feet of water with little or no current. Be sure there is no current deep underwater that is undectable on the surface. Any weather except freezing will do. The search sector is no larger than one square acre. Another option is a long and narrow body of water. The test area allows the dog/handler team enough room to tack (zigzag) back and forth to locate the scent. The dog shows enthusiasm for the job without fear of the boat or water. He moves from one side of the boat to the other to keep the wind blowing into his face. The dog continues to sniff at the water to search for scent. The dog should not lie down in the boat and go to sleep. Once the dog finds the scent, he should give a readable Alert either by barking or by showing by body language that he has found something. Ideally, the dog paws at the water and tries to bite, bark or hang over the side when he finds where the scent is coming up out of the water the strongest. At the time the dog is near or over the diver, the diver comes to the surface and rewards the dog. The dog is friendly toward the diver.

Dogs can and do find bodies in swift water with strong currents. Sometimes these conditions will channel the scent to the surface and the dogs will give good, strong Alerts. Dogs have Alerted almost above a victim in a river that was seven feet above normal, the current traveling south and the wind blowing north. Never underestimate what a dog can detect.

Water practice: Mark O'Brien and Josie. Photo courtesy of Marcia Koenig.

Jib looking for a cadaver.

Handler Sharon Johnson with her German Shepherd, Reva, imprinting on a target scent during cadaver training for Dogs East, Inc.

Chapter 12
Cadaver Training

Before a dog can be trained for cadaver work, he must have mastered wilderness training, as well as small-area or fine-search training. He must thoroughly understand the concept of finding someone. In SAR jargon, "cadaver" refers to any body parts or items used to simulate body parts, as well as the entire corpse. Cadaver searching is very specific area searching. The dog does not run rapidly back and forth across the area. He must work close to the handler.

Cadaver training can be difficult to set up because of the impossibility of training with human body parts. SAR dog trainers have used different objects to simulate a cadaver, such as pig flesh, human teeth (obtained from a dentist), unwashed hair, fingernails, and body fluids. Pig flesh is similar to human flesh. In theory, since pig arteries are successfully transplanted for human arteries, a dog cannot tell the difference. There is a scent on the market, *Pseudocorpse*, made by Sigma, that is supposed to simulate a human cadaver. It is the only scent of its kind that is safe to use. Other scents on the market, such as *Cadaverine*, are considered hazardous material. Exercise caution when handling them.

Many SAR trainers strongly disagree with the use of both cadaver scent and pig flesh and think that only real cadaver and cadaver scent can train the dog. Train with vehicles involved in fatal accidents for real cadaver scent. These vehicles lie in auto junk yards among other, nonfatal accident vehicles. Soil saturated with body fluids from a fatality is also an excellent training site. Such sites have been detected by dogs years after an accident. A dog handler can collect the soil that contains adiposea (a soapy, fatty substance from human flesh) and save it in containers for future use. Soil that has "body burn" on it is especially effective. (Body burn is the black area on the ground where a body has decomposed.) Because each soil type reacts differently, try to collect soil from different areas.

Old graveyards or pauper fields where people have been buried in wooden coffins pose another possibility. Scent will leak into the soil from a decaying corpse, and that soil can be used as cadaver. Often, the dog is not scenting on the body, but the soil that contains the scent.

How you handle and store your cadaver parts is just as important as how and what you use. If you use hair and fingernails (which can be used together), they should be placed in a porous container that allows the scent to come through. An old pair of nylon hose is good. The hose with the hair and fingernails should be stored in an airtight container, such as a *Ziploc* or clear plastic bag with a tie wrap. Wear surgical quality latex gloves, not disposable plastic gloves, when handling any type of body fluid. Gloves protect you from disease present in the body fluid. Teeth can be placed in a jar of water and allowed to sit for a few months at room temperature (out of sight of the squeamish). This produces fluid that can be used. The teeth should be as decayed and as bloody as possible. Other body fluids can be collected and used, such as urine, menstrual fluid, blood and pus. Blood and pus can be captured from used dressings for wounds. These items should be stored in clean containers and can be frozen, but should be thawed for use. Teeth can be frozen if they are not stored in a jar of water. Be sure to mark the packages clearly that contain these items.

A strong consideration when training dogs for cadaver work is the placement of the body parts. If you plan to place the parts yourself for training, be careful that the area does not have your fresh scent and that the area is not obviously disturbed. The dog will key in on these other clues as well as, or instead of, the cadaver scent. Therefore, camouflage the area where the parts are hidden; then, age the area to let the other human scent die down. This is especially important if training green dogs.

Do not let the dog eat the cadaver parts. It is normal for the dog to pick up the object. The dog can easily swallow teeth, fingernails and hair. To protect against this, place the body parts in special containers used to

Handler Teresa MacPherson with her Labrador Retriever, Bama, hitting on target scent in car during cadaver training for Dogs East, Inc.

train drug detection dogs. One such container is a section of rigid PVC pipe with small holes drilled in it to allow scent to escape. Caps on both ends can be removed to put the scented material in the pipe. Put hair, fingernails and teeth in old pantyhose inside the PVC pipe. This prevents the material from falling through the holes in the PVC. Another useful tool is a section of flexible, clear, plastic water hose with crisscross fibers (available in any hardware/building supply store). Inject the scented fluid into the fibers of the hose. Narc bags are also excellent and can be purchased from any catalog that sells K-9 training equipment.

Many SAR dog handlers report that their dogs get depressed and do not give a strong, enthusiastic Alerts when they find cadavers. This is "aversion." When first training your dog, pay close attention to the way the dog behaves and the way he Alerts. (Both female and male dogs will sometimes urinate in the cadaver area as a form of marking.) To distinguish a dead body Alert from a live Find, teach the dog a quiet Alert for cadaver instead of the usual loud, excited Alert used for live Finds. To do this, simply teach the dog to sit, lie down or scratch at the site where the cadaver scent is detected. When deciding which Alert you want to use for cadaver work, bear in mind that police departments want the area disturbed as little as possible.

LEVEL 1: UNDERGROUND VICTIMS

GOAL: To train the dog to find and indicate a buried cadaver.

OBJECTIVE: To teach the dog to locate cadavers as opposed to live victims.

METHOD:

Train in an area without hard soil, such as mud or clay, which does not allow the scent to rise. Don't start training dogs in cold weather with frozen or partially frozen ground. The cadaver specimen must be thawed. Scent will not filter to the top of the soil as well if cold as it does in warm or hot conditions. In the summer, do not work the dog in the heat of the day. Avoid difficult scenting conditions for the beginning exercises and problems. A light breeze is helpful.

There are two ways to handle the cadaver. One is to toss the cadaver part (in a porous container that will allow scent to escape) into heavy brush. This gives the dog a "clean" scent to work from. Or, carefully bury the cadaver in a shallow hole no more than three inches deep under loose soil, vegetation matter, peat moss, etc. Dig four or five dummy holes in the area where you bury the cadaver or the dog will learn to Alert on the disturbed soil. Be sure to age the area for at least 12 hours to let the area become "clean;" this weakens the fresh human scent and allows the cadaver to ripen and become the stronger scent. How long this takes depends on the weather. The hotter the weather, the sooner the site will be ready to use.

When the site is ready, give your dog a command for a close search for cadaver. It should be a different command from the one you use for wilderness searching. If the dog tends to search wide, call him back to you frequently and command him to look in a specific area while you point to the ground. As he puts his head down, praise him and encourage him to keep looking and to stay close (See Additional Commands.)

When you reach the area where the cadaver is hidden, carefully note how your dog reacts. You can teach him a special Alert for cadaver work or just learn to read him well. Keep in mind that for small-area or fine-area search, you should be close enough to your dog to see his Alert. To make up for the dog's depression and disappointment at finding a cadaver, give him a hearty reward including a play reward. It is important to reward the dog as soon as he finds the cadaver—not later after the exercise is finished. Also, give the dog live Finds to keep him "up." Weeks of cadaver work significantly depress the dog and make the whole experience negative.

Once the dog is successfully finding cadaver above the ground, or in a shallow hole, deepen the hole. The deeper you bury the cadaver, the longer it must age in order for the scent to rise. When burying cadaver, dig several false sites so the dog will not learn to look for the holes or dig sites. Keep in mind that dug-up soil gives off a different scent from soil allowed to age.

TEST: Level 1

In weather when the ground is above freezing and the air is 50 degrees or greater, an assistant hides cadaver in a shallow grave no more than six inches deep, consisting of loosely layered dirt. At least four dummy holes are present in the test area. The site has aged for two to four days before the dog/handler team conducts the search. The boundaries of the search area should be no more than 20 to 50 feet square. The dog searches the area thoroughly and continues even after he is tired. The dog gives a readable Alert to the handler when he finds the cadaver site.

LEVEL 2: ABOVE-GROUND HIDDEN CADAVER

GOAL: To lead you to bodies hidden above the ground.

OBJECTIVE: To learn to give an Alert on bodies or concealed body parts.

METHOD:

These exercises should be carefully planned. You are working with inexperienced dogs and asking them to perform conflicting work. Train in a car wrecking yard, a regular junk yard, or another site where there is a great deal of debris. Put your cadaver in a car, under a seat or in a trunk. Keep the area as free of your scent as possible by aging the site for a few days before working the dog. Fine search the area. When the dog starts to show interest in the area where the cadaver is hidden, get excited and encourage the dog.

PROBLEMS:

Some dogs get depressed and work without enthusiasm or show aversion to approaching cadaver. If this happens, switch from cadaver training to live-victim training. It is a good idea to do this anyway to keep the dog "up." Be sure the dog does not injure himself or become frightened during the training. While you do not want to make the work too easy, the dog should not have to spend all of his energy and attention trying to manipulate obstacles. If the dog gets too stressed, he will not want to work.

TEST: Level 2

In weather of 50 degrees or warmer, an assistant hides cadaver above the ground. This can be in a vehicle, wrapped in a rug, in a trash bag, or in a blanket. The cadaver should be allowed to age for at least four to 24 hours. The search area should not exceed 100 feet square. The dog maneuvers in and around the area and shows enthusiasm for the search even when tired. The dog will give a readable Alert when he finds the cadaver.

Riva looking for buried scent source.

Chapter 13
Avalanche Training

Avalanche work is very dangerous. It is a form of disaster work with the added factor of weather conditions to consider. It is important to be instructed by someone trained in the safety requirements necessary to work a high-risk avalanche area.

While avalanche work requires specialized training for the dog/handler team, the concept of finding a buried victim is no different from other disaster work. Because of the dangers involved in avalanche training, the dog should know his Find command and should have been instructed in the digging Alert before avalanche training. Follow the National Ski Patrol procedure for training. It is the basis for the training outlined in this book.

Use people as victims instead of articles of clothing or chemical scent. By always using live victims, you communicate to the dog the urgency to find people, not clothing.

LEVEL 1: PREPARING FOR AVALANCHE TRAINING

GOAL: To familiarize the dog with the modes of transportation used in avalanche situations.

OBJECTIVE: To teach the dog to travel in a vehicle on snow.

METHOD:

Transportation in an avalanche depends on ski lifts, snowmobiles, or other vehicles designed to travel on the snow. At times you must travel on skis with the dog following (or leading). To prepare a dog for avalanche work, practice transporting the dog by every type of vehicle available. Introduce the dog to each mode of transportation while it is stationary and not running. Once the dog is familiar with the vehicle, allow the dog to become accustomed to the vehicle while it is running. When the dog is comfortable with the vehicle running, slowly drive the dog around in the vehicle. With a chair lift, the dog may sit in the chair while it is off, but swaying. Use your common sense. Allow the dog to position himself securely and comfortably.

LEVEL 2: FINDING A VICTIM

NOTE: Because real victims will sometimes make noises, such as moaning and screaming or calling out, it is a good idea to have your victim make noise once in awhile. While it is not necessary for the victim to make noise during each training session, every few training sessions should include some noise. Include moaning, the sound of a personal locator transmitter (such as a SKADI) and calls for help.

GOAL: To have the dog to find a victim placed in a snow cave.

OBJECTIVE: To teach the dog that in snow situations, the victim will be under the snow. He Alerts by digging.

METHOD:
The snow cave must be constructed according to the National Ski Patrol procedures. This includes two

Wilderness work with a Rottweiler. Drawing by Nina Bondarenko.

Border Collie indicates in snow. Drawing by Nina Bondarenko.

Avalanche practice by Nikki Thomas and Tonka. Photo courtesy of Marcia Koenig.

Transport of avalanche dog, Rottweiler, in Europe. Drawing by Nina Bondarenko.

shovelers, two radios (two-way), two avalanche rescue beacons, and six flagging wands for triangulation. The snow cave must be constructed in an area safe from avalanches, clearly marked and weight tested so it will hold the weight of one person on skis or snowshoes standing on top of the cave. This requires that the snow be packed to hold a person's weight. The cave is large enough for the victim to move around and provides adequate air space. Radio contact between the shovelers and the victim must be maintained at all times. If the victim does not respond, dig him out immediately. All personnel involved in the training must wear proper clothing, be well rested, and be alert to any signs of danger.

After the victim is placed in the snow cave, the shoveler radios that the victim is ready. Immediately start to search the area, timing the exercise so the dog arrives at the snow cave in 10 minutes. This allows the scent to rise through the snow.

As soon as the dog gives an Alert, encourage him to dig to the victim. Remove the victim from the snow cave and allow the victim to praise the dog. The total time of the exercise should not be more than 30 minutes. If the dog cannot find the victim in the snow cave by 25 minutes from the time the victim is placed, the exercise should be ended and the victim immediately released from the snow cave.

PROBLEMS:

The dog may have difficulty understanding the idea that a person is under the snow. If this is a problem, allow the dog to see the victim enter the snow cave, in the same manner as the Beginner Runaway for Wilderness Training. When the dog hesitates to go after the victim, the victim calls and teases to encourage the dog to go to him. Once the dog has the idea, advance the training so the dog will not see the victim being hidden.

If the dog does not show enthusiasm for the exercise, the handler can hide and the victim or another person can handle the dog, the same as the Beginning Runaway for wilderness training.

TEST: Level 2

Hide a victim in a snow cave. When the victim is ready, the handler starts his dog. The dog will find the victim within 10 minutes. As soon as the dog finds the snow cave, he digs enthusiastically to reach the victim.

NOTE: In a real avalanche situation in which dogs are called in to look for a victim who has been buried for more than a few days and where the snow is starting to thaw, dogs may give an Alert on the snow runoff, downhill from where the victim is buried, because the scent is carried with the runoff.

Sophie, the United Kingdom's first cave rescue dog, sporting her rescue pack and gear. Drawing by Nina Bondarenko.

Chapter 14
Disaster Training

Although an entire book could be written about disaster training, only the basics are covered in this chapter. No individual should attempt serious disaster training alone. It should be done only in the company of trained professionals with the safety of the SAR team in mind. By its very nature, disaster training is risky. If you wish to train for major disaster situations (usually for national and international response), work with a team that trains specifically for this type of response. Typically, you must respond to a call within a few hours and commit one to two weeks to the incident.

Technically, disaster work involves many different situations that use all aspects of SAR training. For most people, disaster training brings to mind earthquakes, resulting in collapsed buildings. However, disasters include floods, mud slides, avalanches, and fires, as well as collapsed buildings. Units usually train for situations that would most likely occur in their areas. Some units respond nationally and/or internationally and train for all kinds of disasters.

As with any other aspect of search work, there are as many ideas and opinions about disaster work as there are handlers. However, there is one facet of disaster work on which almost everyone agrees. Dogs used for disaster work should be controllable from a distance and take directional commands.

Disaster work requires the handler to have special training in many subjects. In handling hazardous material, identify the materials, and take extra precautions to prevent your dog from touching them. Your dog should not walk in, drink, or breathe anything that may contain dangerous substances. On a real disaster mission this may be easier said than done, but all possible precautions must be taken to keep both you and your dog safe.

You need a special awareness of structural dangers. The disaster respondent often works around unsafe and structurally damaged or unsound buildings. No amount of training can truly simulate the actual disaster. The SAR dog handler and other rescue personnel face many problems unique to an actual disaster, such as fuel leakage, vapor leakage (gas and other harmful fumes), food and water contamination, unpleasant odors, dust, dirt, and noises, which may include loud machinery, general confusion, and the cries and screaming of people and animals. The emotional atmosphere of disaster rescue work cannot be simulated. Because of the high emotional impact of disaster rescue work, special debriefing teams have been trained in Critical Incident Stress Management. These teams help disaster workers cope with reactions to destruction, injury and death.

All the elements of the disaster affect how your dog will work as well as his ability to detect scent. When you consider the difficulty, the dogs will amaze you.

The best you can do to prepare the dog for a disaster is to simulate what the dog will encounter in any situation. But first you must teach the basics. Start with wilderness training and become proficient. This gives the dog a pleasant place to learn the concept that he must find someone. Most SAR dog handlers use their dogs for wilderness as well as other types of search work. Next, you must master the Additional Commands, focusing on Wait, Go In A Specific Direction, Look, Climb A Ladder, Crawl Through A Culvert, Slick and Unstable Surfaces, Turn Around, Moving Surfaces and the Closed End Tunnel. Directional commands and agility exercises should be taught before the dog is asked to work rubble or debris piles. The Alert is also taught first with the use of an Enzler Box constructed from a large piece of conduit or sewer pipe or similar training device.

The dog must have a strong readable Alert. Due to the nature of the work, the dog does not do a Re-find when doing disaster work; instead, he gives his Alert at the point where the scent is detectable. The dog must not Alert on anything but human bodies, alive or dead. Most dogs give a different Alert on dead bodies; you must know your dog's dead-body Alert. Sometimes the intensity of the Alert is the only variation.

At this writing, all units throughout the world use the Bark Alert for disaster work. A Digging Alert in these situations can trigger a cave-in or further injure the victim, and is not acceptable. The dog must not Alert on furniture, clothing, animals, food (both human and dog) nor the feces of humans or animals. Therefore, a food reward is not good for disaster work. Do not condition the dog to expect and eat tidbits at the disaster site. For safety reasons, do not encourage a retrieve game as your dog's reward. At a real disaster site, you would not want your dog running back and forth over hazardous terrain. A good method of reward is a tug toy and a game of tug with the dog after he has completed his exercise. If you are on a rubble pile with your dog, after he has given his Alert and been called off the problem, you can put the tug toy in the dog's mouth and let him carry it off the rubble pile. Play tug-of-war once you are off the rubble pile.

Training Site

Finding a disaster training site is not easy. While it must simulate a real disaster as much as possible, it should also be safe to work on, under, and around the site. Do not forget, people and dogs training on-site are learning and are not experienced search teams. There should be room for error. Exercise utmost safety when placing and hiding victims. Victims should never be placed in a situation in which debris could fall and injure them. The ideal site should be made of concrete rubble, but wooden pallets, boxes, bricks, pipes, logs, or abandoned buildings with debris in disarray is satisfactory. Most large buildings are made of reinforced concrete; therefore, the dog should have some exposure to concrete debris. The search site should contain debris arranged to allow the dog to practice his agility and build determination.

At some point in the training, it is a good idea to place smoke bombs in various parts of the debris pile to imitate scent, so you can learn how the scent filters through debris and rubble in various weather conditions and times of day. Do this in intact buildings as well. Scent behaves differently in a disaster situation from the way it does in the wilderness. In a real disaster, the rubble piles generate their own air currents unique to each pile.

For safety reasons, dogs must work the rubble piles without collars or vests. Also, in many cases, the handler does not go onto the rubble pile. Therefore, the dog must be able to work apart from the handler, directed by hand signals, whistles or voice commands.

Level 1: Buried Victim

GOAL: To teach the dog that bodies can be under the ground or under debris.

OBJECTIVE: To have the dog find and Alert on a person hidden in debris.

METHOD:

If the dog has been successfully trained in wilderness search techniques, he can probably start disaster work with someone he does not know. If the dog is unsure or hesitant, the handler may have to be the victim. At first, just barely bury the victim and be sure the dog cannot be hurt finding the victim. This is very important, because if the dog is injured or frightened, he may resist finding people in the environment in which he has been hurt. On the other hand, if the experience is pleasant and "up," the dog's desire and enthusiasm will be heightened. In the beginning, it is important for the dog to see the victim come out of the hiding place, to meet the victim and to have the victim praise the dog.

After the dog has had strong successes and he can reach the victim readily, frustrate him by placing the victim where the dog cannot reach him easily. Encourage the dog to bark. Use a tug toy to allow the victim to play with the dog. The dog can help pull the victim out of the hole once he has found the victim. Once the victim is out, the handler can take over the play reward. To do this, set up the problems carefully.

Marcia Koenig and Bear searching in rubble after a tornado in Wichita Falls, Texas, 1979. Photo courtesy of Bob Koenig.

*Handler Patty Depp and Rubble, a Golden Retriever, practicing
disaster training for the Ross Township SAR group.*

*Handler Shirley Hammond and Cinnamon (Doberman Pinscher) practicing
disaster training for the California Rescue Dog Association. Dog is indicating a
covered victim.*

Marcia Koenig's dog Orca practicing disaster training.
Photo courtesy of Bob Koenig.

Ira, a Doberman Pinscher, working a disaster drill with handler M. Limoger. Photo courtesy of
SARDAA.

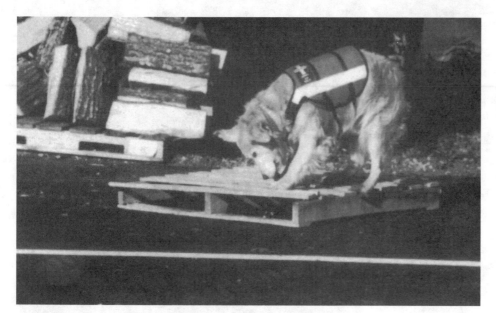

Mat, digging at a dead scent source.

Asta, a Malinwa, working a large rubble area with handler K. George. Photo courtesy of SARDA.

The Enzler Box excites a dog. It is constructed from a large piece of conduit or sewer pipe. Hide the victim in a concrete pipe buried in a hillside. After the victim is hidden, cover the front with something like plywood, and put loose sand or dirt in front of that. The victim should have something that belongs to the dog. The object should be an item the dog likes and wants very much. The pipe should be open enough for the victim to get fresh air and for the dog to see the victim in the pipe but not be able to get through the opening. The dog is given the Find command in the area of the pipe. When the dog finds the victim, the victim teases the dog with the object to get the dog to bark and dig to get to him. Also, give the dog the command Dig when he starts to dig. This names the action so that he will dig on command. After a short time, when the dog is barking and digging, the victim pushes the plywood aside and lets the dog come to him. In some cases, you will have to remove the plywood. Encourage the dog during the whole process to get the dog excited.

If a concrete pipe is not available, use whatever will achieve the same results. The dog must be able to find the victim, but be prevented from reaching him right away. Take care that the dog will not be hurt or frightened. If the victim becomes claustrophobic, discontinue the problem until a new victim can be found.

Vary the training sites as much as possible or the dog will learn just where to go to find his victim. The beginning disaster problem can be handled in an area with a victim hidden in a small rubble pile. Sigma also markets a *Stressed Person* scent that is an excellent aid for disaster training.

PROBLEMS:

The dog may not get excited or frustrated enough to give a strong Alert. If this happens, let the dog see the victim enter the tunnel or rubble pile. Be sure enough scent escapes from the tunnel to turn the dog on. When the dog goes up to the tunnel to try to get to the victim, go with him, showing a great deal of excitement and start digging also. If the dog does not get very excited, the victim can tease the dog with a toy or by calling to the dog. Since you do not want the dog to associate eating with the disaster site, do not use food as a reward. At a real disaster, food will be part of the disaster debris and you do not want the dog to pick up food and eat it.

TEST: Level 1

Hide a victim in a pipe or under debris. Send the dog to the area and give the Find command. The handler must be able to tell the tester the type of Alert the dog will give. The dog finds the victim, shows enthusiasm and stays at the point where the scent is exiting the test site until the handler either brings the victim out or the dog is released from the exercise.

Bear in mind that if you have used the training site more than once during the training exercise, the dog may check out residual scent but not give an active Alert.

LEVEL 2: BODIES ONLY

GOAL: To proof the dog against giving Alerts on anything except humans.

OBJECTIVE: To ensure that the dog ignores anything that is not a live or dead human body.

METHOD:

Once the dog can find live victims in debris reliably, set up situations with distractions. Set up two to four hiding places in a debris pile or in the disaster search training area. Put food in one, clothing in another and a victim in another. Be sure to mark which hiding place has the person and which have the other objects. Send the dog out on the Find command and follow him closely. If the dog Alerts on the wrong hiding place, give him a stern No and direct him toward the victim. When he finds the victim and gives his alert, praise the dog enthusiastically.

As the dog masters the idea that he should not Alert on anything but people, you can add all of the distractions mentioned in the beginning of this chapter. Be sure to include the odors of food, feces, furniture, clothing, and chemicals, such as bleach and ammonia. Human distractions can be other workers, police, fire personnel, onlookers, etc. Place smoke bombs or small fires adjacent to the site. Provide the sound of rescue traffic, equipment, chain saws, etc. Put a small animal such as a chicken, a cat, or a rat in a cage and hide it so the dog learns to ignore animals.

At this stage of the training, the handler must be careful not to encourage the dog to give false Alerts, or to teach the dog to Alert on the wrong scent. Knowing where your victim is located and where his scent is rising will help to avoid this problem.

TEST A: Level 2

Place one to four victims in a debris pile in a simulated disaster situation. There will be at least one victim and three false sites baited with distractions, including noise, odors, and buried distractions. Send the dog with the Find command. The handler searches his sector and reports what the dog has found to the tester. The handler marks those places where the dog has indicated a human body. If the dog has more than one false Alert out of four test locations, he fails the test.

TEST B: Level 2

The test will be conducted as in Test 2A but with no victim hidden in the debris. The dog must clear the area and the handler must determine that there is no victim in his sector. The test area has at least four baited sites. After this test, give the dog a short problem with a victim so the dog can have a live Find. The problem can be a wilderness problem; the main objective is to let the dog have a Find.

LEVEL 3: ADVANCED DISASTER WORK

GOAL: To practice all of the skills needed for disaster work.

METHOD:

During the practices, after the dog has reliably performed Levels 1 and 2, start to practice the directional commands. This is not the time to teach the dog the directional commands; it is the time to put the training to practical use. Send the dog on debris away from you, to your right and left. Make sure you can send your dog at least 50 feet. While the dog is on debris, practice the Back and Wait commands. Be sure the dog is required to crawl through tunnels at least two feet high and four feet long. The dog should go into a tunnel at least 25 feet long with no visible exit. Practice with a tunnel that has right angle turns.

TEST: Level 3:

To test your dog's advanced work, you need to set up every situation you can manage. While looking for his victim, have the dog maneuver through debris and objects, including tunnels. After ample practice, the dog will become confident and experienced enough to handle an actual disaster.

Chapter 15
Small-Area Search or Fine Search

Use the small-area or fine search when looking for a small or buried object. The search can be for articles or a cadaver, including buried victims at a disaster site or for body parts. Commonly, the dog must sniff every inch of the area. Because of the energy expended in fine search, the dog will not be able to search a very large area at one time. How long he can search depends on the individual dog. Some dogs tire quicker than others, causing their scent capabilities to shut down or become unreliable. The stress and intensity of the search can cause fatigue. The dogs need frequent rests; other dogs may be used at the same time.

Often, the handler can send the dog into the area to do a hasty search to see if the dog can locate the specific area in which to concentrate the search effort. If the dog comes up with nothing, then the fine-search technique must be used. Each handler has his own method for conducting a fine search, but the dog must sniff each inch of the area. Some handlers set up string lines in a grid pattern, placing each grid string about 12 feet apart. This method allows the handler to work the dog on a standard six-foot leash, moving the dog from side to side.

Another method is to cross-grid (or double grid) an area. Cover the area in one direction, such as north and south, and then cover the same area in grids from east to west. This method ensures covering every bit of the area.

Practice the fine-search technique using articles and cadaver. For most dogs, tracking training helps master the fine-search technique because it teaches the dog to work with his nose to the ground looking for human scent. Teaching the dog to track prepares the dog for what is expected when he puts on his tracking harness.

FINE-SEARCH TECHNIQUE

GOAL: To teach the dog the concept of fine searching.

OBJECTIVE: To enable the dog to fine search an area for cadaver, objects, footprints, etc.

METHOD:
Using either cadaver parts or an article, hide something in a small area of about 15 to 20 feet square. Give the dog a command for fine searching and encourage him to work slowly with his nose to the ground. You may need to work the dog on-leash to teach him not to range as far in fine searching as in wilderness searching. The object hidden should not be visible to the dog and can be buried or hidden near debris, such as leaves, grass clippings, etc. When the dog finds the object, praise him and give him a food or play reward.

Once the dog learns the fine search and reliably and deliberately works with his nose to the ground, practice working the dog between string-lines, used to rope off an area for gridsearching. Use sticks and string to section the area into alleyways. The dog and handler work the alleyways to fine search the area.

TEST 1
Set the test in any terrain, in a section about 20 feet square. The handler gives the dog the fine-search command and the dog works every inch of the ground, nose down, looking for a hidden object. The dog shows enthusiasm and keeps his nose to the ground. The dog may rest and lift his head, but he must return to the search and not miss any inch of the section.

Dog performing a small-area search in a sectional with string lines. Drawing by Marcus Adkins.

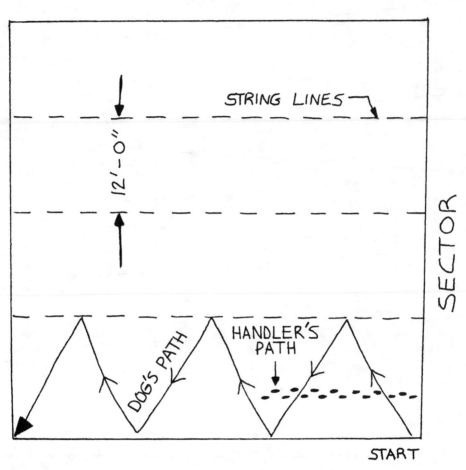

Fine search with string lines. Dividing a small sector with string lines helps to show the dog that he is doing a fine search. It also helps you identify where you need to search. Drawing by Joseph T. McNichol.

TEST 2

Set the problem as above, with four or five objects hidden in the area. The handler starts the dog in one corner of the sector and directs his dog to search the entire area using a grid pattern.

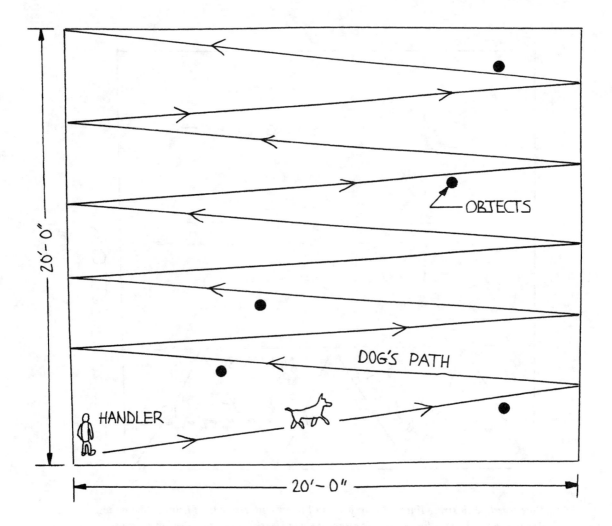

Small objects are randomly placed in the area. The handler will direct the dog to search the area using a grid technique. Drawing by Joseph T. McNichol.

Chapter 16
Evidence Search

Most dogs have no problem finding articles laden with human scent. There are two types of article work the dog must do. In one, the dog is asked to look for a specific article of evidence search. Often, this occurs when a weapon or object has been discarded in a suspect area. The other is when an article is discovered while looking for the victim. In most cases, the articles are clothing, discarded food wrappers, or other objects purposely or accidentally dropped by the lost person. Of course, you always look for articles and clues on a search; the chances of the victim being in your search sector are very slim. Your dog must alert on articles whether you give him the command to do so or not.

In a wilderness situation, the dog should be trained to alert on anything that has human scent on it. Therefore, you must also teach a command to look for articles rather than victims.

In all evidence searches, the dog must not pick up the article he has found. Rather than touch or move the article, the dog gives a Bark Alert or lies down next to the article. The dog must not mouth the article as the police may want to send the article to the lab for analysis. They do not want dog saliva on it. The position and location of the article can also be very important, so it must not be disturbed. In a wilderness setting, an article verified as belonging to the victim can mean a shift in the PLS (Point Last Seen) and in the search effort. If an airscenting dog found the article and the article is not touched by anyone, a tracking dog can be scented on the article to track the victim from that point.

Riva locating a "hanging suicide."

Level 1: Beginning Article

GOAL: To teach the dog to give an Alert on an article.

OBJECTIVE: To teach the dog the article search command, and to search for articles.

METHOD:

Either you or the victim toss an article into a field of moderate brush or grass, upwind from the starting point. The article should not be visible to the dog after it lands, although the dog should see the object being tossed. It helps to tease the dog with the object to get his attention focused on it.

While the dog is excited and at his peak of interest, give him the command to search for the article. The article-search command is different from the victim-search command. Some handlers use Find for people and Seek for objects. Encourage the dog to run after the article. When the dog reaches the article, either have him sit by the article and/or bark as an Alert (the method preferred by most SAR dog handlers), or have the dog return to you, giving the found Alert, and do a Re-find.

Many people think that because the dog is doing a fine search, the Re-find is not necessary. They reserve the Re-find for live victims only. This is your decision. Once the dog finds the article and either you reach him or he gives an Alert and Re-find, give him a reward for finding the article. Continue this exercise until the dog understands that the command means to find an article, not a victim.

PROBLEMS:

Most dogs have been taught to find a person before article training; therefore, they may want to run to the victim instead of to the article. When this happens, gently lead the dog to the article, and give him the command for article search as you point to the article. Praise him when he looks at the article and sniffs it. If the victim is in sight of the dog and is too distracting to the dog, toss the article yourself. Once the dog understands the article search command, you can have someone else place the article for you.

If the dog seems too confused by the whole exercise, teach the dog in stages:

1. The dog learns to run after the article.
2. The dog runs to the article and lies down or barks next to the article.

For dogs who are going to be trained in disaster work, a more passive Alert is better because the disaster area will be littered with human-scented articles and you do not want your dog to do a Re-find over unstable surfaces.

TEST: Level 1

With the dog watching, the handler tosses an object upwind, about 20 feet from the dog, into an area where the article cannot be readily seen by the dog once it lands. When the article lands, the handler sends the dog to find it. The dog locates the article and gives his Article Alert.

Level 2: Hidden Article

GOAL: To have the dog search for an article.

OBJECTIVE: To train the dog to find articles that he did not see tossed or hidden.

METHOD:

Once the dog can successfully find an article he sees being tossed, start hiding an article that the dog does not see being placed. Be sure the article is placed upwind from the starting point. Give the command to search for the article and start to work the area. This is a fine search: keep the dog close to you and do not allow him to range as far as you would in a wilderness setting. If the vegetation allows, the dog should remain within your sight. The object is to have the dog search the area thoroughly. Teach this by having him stay closer to you and work a tighter grid pattern.

TEST: Level 2

The handler has someone place an article within a small area, about 200 feet square, without the dog watching. After the article is placed, the handler starts the dog on a fine search. Do not cross the trail left by the person who has hidden the article. The dog searches thoroughly, covering the area in a fine search. The dog finds the article and gives an Alert.

PART III
GOING BEYOND

A SAR dog must learn how to move over, under and on all types of debris. Handler Joy Zerfing and her dog Boots (German Shepherd) practicing agility training for Dogs East group.

Chapter 17
Additional Commands for the SAR Dog

Many of the additional commands come from agility exercises. However, there is one important difference between agility and SAR work: agility work is often rapid and showy. In SAR, you do not want the dog to search quickly. Many of the SAR exercises prepare the dog for collapsed building and rubble disaster searches. This requires slow, deliberate movement. In a disaster, if the dog rushes, it could mean injury or death for the dog, handler, or others. Strong control and judgment are required for both the dog and handler. The dog must respond to the handler's command and must maneuver safely out of sight of the handler.

THE BACK COMMAND

GOAL: To teach the dog to backup rather than turn around.

OBJECTIVE: The dog learns to think about the placement of his hind feet and to move backwards. This command means the dog is to back away from whatever he has focused on, or whatever he is looking at.

METHOD

Place low objects, such as picnic benches that are about shoulder height to the dog, in a parallel position. They must not topple easily, and if they wobble have two assistants stand outside the benches to support them. Avoid frightening the dog; he should be able to see above the objects and not feel too confined. Place the objects far enough apart to discourage the dog from turning around. First, walk the dog forward through the barriers to familiarize him with them. Don't let the dog jump up on the objects, since this will encourage him to jump out rather than to backup. Once the dog is comfortable, stand him between them with his nose even with the end.

Place yourself directly in front of the dog with your body almost touching the dog's nose. Avoid startling the dog. Once the dog is relaxed enough to pay attention to you, give him the command Back (or whatever word you choose to use), and start to walk slowly forward into the dog. Do not rush him or he may panic and try to jump out. Give him time to think about what you are asking and to decide to back up. Encourage the dog as you move forward and guide him, if necessary, to back up rather than turn around or jump out.

Some dogs can learn this exercise without the aid of the benches. Just stand in front of the dog, give the Back command, and walk forward slowly. The dog will back up as you move. Once the dog is backing up with no signs of stress, remove the objects and give him the Back command.

TEST

The dog handler positions the dog between two objects and gives the dog the Back command. The dog moves backwards confidently and deliberately.

THE WAIT COMMAND

GOAL: To teach the dog he must freeze for a short period wherever he is at the time of the command.

OBJECTIVE: To have the dog stop in his tracks and wait for a further command.

METHOD

This command is a variation of the Stay or Stand command. The difference is the application and position the dog is required to maintain. For the Stay command, the dog remains in one position, sitting or lying down. With the Wait command, the dog stops in whatever position he is in and waits for the next command. This command is especially useful when a dog must negotiate unstable rubble or debris.

Train where you have access to a tree or pole of some sort. Tie a long rope to the dog's collar and tell the dog to stay near the pole or tree. Loop the rope around the tree once so that it moves freely when the dog moves. You and your dog form a "U" with the rope tied around the dog's collar, going around the tree and coming back to you. There should be enough rope to allow the dog to reach you while you are still holding the rope. Walk as far away from the dog as possible. Call the dog. As the dog comes to you, give a Wait command and gently stop the dog from moving forward by pulling on the rope. As soon as the dog stops, praise him. Then call the dog again and let the dog come to you, praising heartily.

When practicing this exercise, do not give the dog the Wait command at the same place each time. Vary the exercise as much as possible. It is all right to give the dog more than one Wait command in each recall. You can teach the dog a hand signal by giving it when you say Wait. As the dog learns the Wait, use it in different situations so he becomes familiar with the command.

PROBLEMS

The dog may come so fast that is difficult to stop him before he reaches you. Generally, after a few tries, the dog slows down and anticipates the Wait command. If he doesn't, then a longer rope allows you time to slow him down. Initially, the dog may sit or lie down when he gets the Wait Command. Ignore the position and allow him to do what is comfortable. As he gets used to the command, he learns to wait in the position safest and most comfortable for him. The command for this exercise is different from the commands used for obedience work. The dog learns through practice that Wait means to freeze in his place and not to drop on recall or stay in one position.

TEST

The handler puts the dog in a sit-stay and walks about 50 feet from the dog. When the handler is ready, he calls the dog. As the dog comes toward the handler, he give the dog the Wait command and the dog stops. The handler then calls the dog allows him to come in.

THE TURN-AROUND COMMAND

NOTE: Dogs tend always to turn either right or left just as right- and left-handed people do.

GOAL: To have the dog turn around on a narrow surface.

OBJECTIVE: To teach the dog not to bolt, but to turn slowly with thought about where he is placing his feet.

METHOD

The dog should be taught to walk a board before doing this exercise. Once the dog successfully walks across a narrow (4 inches) board, place a six- to 12-inch board a few feet off the ground using cinder blocks or bricks to support it. You and an assistant stand on either side of the dog. With the dog on a wait or stay, give him a Turn command. As you give the command, turn his head slowly so that he must turn around. Get the dog to think about where his feet are going. If he jumps off, put him back on the board and start over.

PROBLEMS

Some dogs jump off the board. Because of their size and strength, it is difficult to keep them from jumping. Try putting the board along a wall so the dog must turn toward you. Give him the Turn command and block the dog with your body so he must turn around as you guide him with his leash. The dog is much easier to control if you use a head harness.

TEST

The handler directs the dog to step up on a board and wait. Then the handler walks the dog forward until he just reaches the end of the board. At this time, the handler gives the dog the command to Turn Around. The dog turns around deliberately without jumping off the board.

THE GO-TO COMMAND

The Go To is a variation of the report command used for courier and message dogs during World War II. In its original form, two handlers were used for each dog. The dog regarded both handlers as his masters and obeyed each equally. Training did not start until the dog accepted this arrangement. The training techniques were very similar to those used for SAR. The military training required the dog to report with a handkerchief tied around his neck to give him the feeling he was bringing something to the other handler. Each handler would use his own handkerchief. This procedure was also used to prepare the dog for carrying the message cylinder, which would be required later in training. As the dog learned to run back and forth on command between his two handlers, distance and obstacles were added to simulate the battlefield. The message/courier dog was also required to transport pigeons, telephone wire, ammunition and whatever else was needed. The main variation between military training and SAR work is that the SAR dog is taught to Go To several different assistants, but must always return to the same handler.

For all three Go commands, the handler should avoid using the dog's name. Most people teach their dogs to come using the dog's name. Therefore, using the dog's name could confuse the dog.

If you need to use both the Go To and the Go commands, you may want to use a different word, such as Away or Way to avoid confusing the dog.

GOAL: The dog must learn that he is to Go To a specific person on command.

OBJECTIVE: To teach the dog to go directly to a named person and identify the person by any means necessary.

METHOD

Use an assistant that the dog knows, such as a family member. You and the assistant stand about 25 feet apart. As the handler gives the command Go To *name of assistant*, the assistant calls the dog. When the dog runs to the assistant, the assistant gives the dog hearty praise or a reward. The assistant plays with the dog for a few minutes before sending the dog back. The dog should not get the feeling he is being sent away for misbehaving or that he is unwanted, but rather that he has accomplished his task. Then the assistant gives the dog the Go To *name of handler* command and encourages the dog to return to you as you call him. It should not take the dog long to learn that he is to report to the person he is told to go to. As the dog learns the command, increase the distance between yourself and the assistant, and use people the dog does not know well. Be sure that before each training session the dog is introduced to the assistant. For SAR purposes, you can use a generic name for the assistant, such as Go To Helper. The main purpose of this exercise is to teach the dog that he must go back and forth between you and the victim. It is not the object of this exercise for the dog to find a specific person.

TEST

    In an area that is open or has light brush, the handler places an assistant about 50 feet away. The assistant is visible to the dog. The handler gives the dog the Go To command and sends him to the assistant. The dog goes directly to the assistant who praises the dog and plays with him for a minute. Then the assistant gives the dog the Go To command to return to the handler. Again, the dog proceeds directly to the handler, who also praises the dog and plays with him.

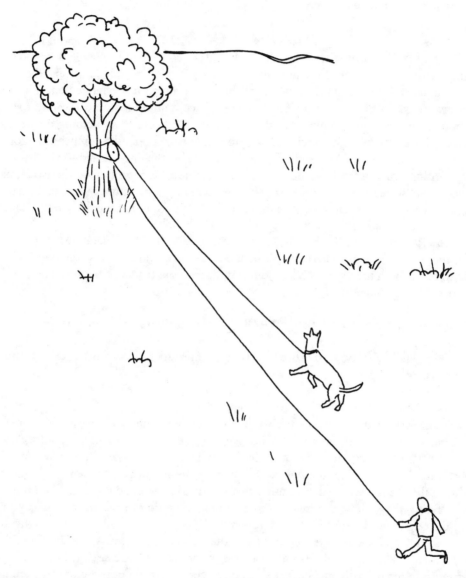

By using a pulley and/or a tree, you can teach the dog to leave you on command. Drawing by Joseph T. McNichol.

THE GO COMMAND

GOAL: To teach the dog to move away from the handler.

OBJECTIVE: To have the dog learn that upon being given the command Go, he moves away ahead of the handler on the way to an object—not to a human. This is the difference between the Go command and the go to command. The Go command is used more to direct the dog in a disaster, and is often coupled with the find command. Sometimes the Go command is given with no ultimate target apparent to the dog.

METHOD I

This exercise teaches the dog that he must move away from his handler, usually in front of him. At this point, the only direction the dog is to move is directly away from the handler in a straight line.

Set up the exercise in an area with good ground visibility, low grass, hard surface, etc. The dog sits at heel or so that he can watch the area in front of you. Unless you have total control over your dog, have him on-leash.

Food works well as a reward for this exercise. It's best to use food instead of toys because most people use toys and sticks in fetch games. For the Go, you don't want the dog to return to you until he is called. The dog will not pick up food and bring it back to you, but he may be tempted to bring back objects he is used to retrieving. Tease the dog with a small piece of food, then toss the food in front of the dog about 10 feet away. With some dogs, you may have to give the command as you throw the food. In the beginning, don't make the dog wait; you want the dog to go when his interest is at its peak. When the dog reaches the food, give him hearty verbal praise and place him in a sit-stay. Walk to the dog and praise him with a pat on the head and a "good dog." Once the dog gets the idea of the game, increase the distance that you toss the food and require him to wait a few seconds before you tell him Go. As the dog learns that on Go he is to move away from you, stop using food as a reward and concentrate on verbal commands and praise. Be sure to give the dog a wait, stay or some sort of stop command when he reaches the food or the target. The dog will not assume that when he reaches the goal he is to wait. You do not want the dog to get in the habit of going to the point, turning around and then running back to you.

METHOD 2

Use an assistant and a rope about 100 feet long or more. Have the assistant sit with one end of the rope (ideally behind something like a fence) where he will not be the focus of the dog's attention. Position yourself away from the assistant as far as the rope will allow. With the other end of the rope attached to the dog, and the dog sitting at your side, start to walk toward the assistant and give the dog the Go command. At first, the dog will tend to heel with you. Encourage the dog to move away from you by extending your arm and repeating Go. Slow down while the assistant pulls gently on the rope to encourage the dog to move away from you. As the dog moves away, give an upbeat Go command and hearty verbal praise. When the dog reaches the assistant by the fence, he will stop. Give the dog a sit-stay command and walk to him. Praise the dog and give him a treat, if you choose. Holding the dog by the collar, walk him back to the end of the rope and repeat the exercise.

METHOD 3

This technique is the same as Method 2, except that it requires a pulley instead of an assistant. Be sure to place the pulley about three to four feet above the dog's head and attach it to an object that will not fall or move. Bear in mind that you must start at half the distance because the rope will be doubled. To compensate, move back as the dog moves forward to increase the distance between you and the dog. With the dog in heel position, give him the Go command as you slowly move forward and pull gently on the rope. Decrease your speed as you allow the dog to get further ahead. Be sure to reassure the dog if he seems confused and praise him for moving away from you. As the dog leaves you, start to move backwards to gain the maximum distance between you and the dog. Once the dog reaches the pulley, give him a sit-stay command. Return to the dog, reward him, and lead him by the collar back to the beginning. Repeat the exercise.

PROBLEMS

Sometimes as you start to move backwards, the dog will stop and try to follow you, thinking you have shifted direction. If the dog does this, move forward again giving the dog the Go command while gently pulling on the rope. If the dog refuses to move away from you as you move backwards, try a different method; or, do not move backwards. Remain at the point where you stopped moving forward. Focus on getting the dog to leave you while you remain stationary. Once he understands the command and does it, you can work to increase the distance.

METHOD 4

Use a fenced area that is large enough to increase distance as you progress through the problem. Put the dog in a sit-stay and walk across the enclosed area, placing a hat, jacket, or other visible object with food across the field. Walk back to the dog and send him out to the object. When the dog reaches the object, command the dog down or sit the dog next to it.

PROBLEMS

If the dog is reluctant to leave you to go to the object, or seems confused, place the object closer to the dog, upwind so he can smell the food. Encourage him to go ahead of you by pointing at the object and starting to walk toward it. Usually, it will only take once or twice for the dog to get the idea that there is food he can have.

TEST

The handler starts with the dog in heel position. The handler gives the dog the Go command and the dog moves away from the handler in a straight line until told to stop. Give the wait command; the dog stays there until the handler either calls the dog back or goes to the dog. The dog leaves the handler confidently, without hesitation.

Go in a Specific Direction

GOAL: To teach the dog to move forward away from his handler, either in a specific direction or to be redirected while away from the handler.

OBJECTIVE: To get the dog to leave the handler and move in the specified direction until he is told to stop.

METHOD

There are many ways to execute this exercise. The ultimate goal is to have the dog move to an area you indicate. Some people use a specific signal for right and left direction, either a hand signal, a whistle tone or a verbal command. Some people use a verbal command to have the dog move away from them combined with a hand signal or whistle to show which direction the dog should go. Whatever you use, be consistent. It is important to wait until the dog knows the command for one direction before you teach the command for the other direction.

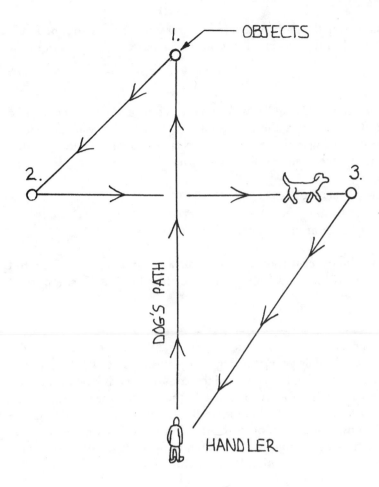

OBJECTS

1.

2.

3.

DOG'S PATH

HANDLER

Go in a Specific Directiion: 1) Dog is sent to center object; 2) Dog is sent to object 2 or 3; Dog is sent from object 2 or 3 to opposite object; 4) Dog is recalled. Drawing by Joseph T. McNichol.

Give the dog the Go command and point in the direction you want the dog to go. Or, give the Go command and place your hand on the side of the dog's face so his vision is blocked on one side. The dog is to go to the site he can see, or move in the direction his head is pointing.

Another method is to give the Right or Left command and direct the dog by moving your body in the direction he is to go.

You may use the pulley as described in the Go exercise, but stand at an angle so the dog must move to the right or left when he feels the pull of the rope.

You may use food as an indicator. Toss the food in the direction you want the dog to go and give the command.

Whichever method you use, the technique for teaching the dog is the same. Give the dog the command and encourage him to go away from you in the direction indicated. If you have taught the dog the Go command first, he will understand he is to move away from you. All you have to do now is to make him understand he is to move in a specific direction. It helps if you have a highly visible object for the dog to go to. A wooden pallet or something obvious will give the dog a goal to reach at first. Once the dog has reached the spot, it is equally important for you to give him a wait or some type of halt command. The dog must learn that he is to go until he is told to stop.

When the dog masters the concept, stop using the props and have him move into a field until he is told to stop. After much practice, the dog will head in the specific direction you indicate, whether it is to the extreme right or left or just straight.

TEST

The handler and dog will start in heel position. The handler will send the dog to an object straight ahead to an obvious target. Once the dog reaches the object, give the command to stop. The dog waits there until told to move. At that point, the handler directs the dog to the second obvious target. Again, the dog is told to wait, and then is sent to the third object. Finally, the handler calls the dog back.

THE LOOK COMMAND

GOAL: To teach the dog to look in a specific area or spot.

OBJECTIVE: This exercise is similar to the go command. Use Look when the dog is instructed to search a specific spot, such as a clump of brush, a hole or any confined area. This is part of small-area-search work.

METHOD

This exercise works well with food as a reward. Place a small piece of food on the ground and then point to it close enough so you can almost touch the food, while giving the dog the command to Look. After three or four sessions with food, add a search article. Once the dog has associated the command with looking at a spot you point out, eliminate the food and use articles, such as toys or clothing. As the dog gets the idea, he can be directed to look at and sniff the scent from a footprint. You should get the dog accustomed to going into confined areas to look. It is important to stop using food as soon as the dog learns the Look command. He must learn that he is looking for scent and search-related objects. The dog must understand he is looking for an article or scent and not just doing the exercise on your whim. If the dog understands Look, he will stop looking when commanded.

TEST

An assistant places two objects in an area about 10-feet square. The first object is hidden by an object, such as grass or brush. The second object should be too small to see right away, like a coin. The handler gives the dog the Look command and points to the ground. The handler encourages the dog to continue looking in a fine-search technique until the dog finds the object. The dog searches enthusiastically without the need to be commanded again.

THE CLIMB-A-LADDER COMMAND

GOAL: To teach the dog to climb up and down a ladder on command and with confidence.

OBJECTIVE: To develop balance and to teach the dog to be aware of where he is placing his feet, specifically focusing on rear feet placement.

METHOD

To start this exercise, you need special equipment. In the beginning, use a ladder with flat steps instead of round rungs and with steps on both sides. As the dog gains confidence, you may progress to using round rungs.

Start by letting the dog look at and examine the ladder. As soon as the dog feels comfortable, pat the steps with your hand, command Climb and encourage the dog to go up. As assistant stands on one side of the dog while you stand on the other. Use food as an incentive if necessary. When teaching the dog to go up a ladder, it is very important that the dog not panic and fall. Both you and the assistant must be ready to support the dog.

Most dogs will put their front feet on the ladder but will stop when their hind feet leave the ground. Gently place the dog's hind feet, one at a time, on the bottom rung of the ladder. As soon as the dog is comfortable, urge him to take the next step, all the time giving the Climb command. If the dog rushes and tries to jump to the top, use the leash to hold him back. The dog who jumps is not going to think about the placement of his hind feet. He needs awareness of the hind feet for balance. The fearful dog must be encouraged and praised a great deal as he gains confidence. Sometimes it helps if you get on the top of the ladder and encourage the dog to come up. Take care to teach the dog to go down the opposite side of the ladder. The dog should both climb and go down slowly with control.

PROBLEMS

Some dogs have trouble getting over their fear of climbing ladders. This is due, in part, to feeling unsafe because they can see through the steps of the ladder. For dogs who show persistent reluctance to climb a ladder, tape tissue paper over the back of the steps to give the illusion that the steps are closed. Once the dog gains confidence in climbing the ladder, he will not be concerned if the paper is there or not.

Another reason for fearfulness is that people use slides in playgrounds to teach dogs to climb ladders. This is all right if a dog is confident. But for the more fearful or younger dog, the slide down can be frightening. If you use a playground slide, be sure the metal slide part is not hot and that the dog does not become frightened by the slippery surface.

TEST

At the Climb command, the dog climbs a ladder confidently, slowly and carefully. He displays awareness of where he is placing his feet.

THE CRAWLING-THROUGH-A-TUNNEL COMMAND

NOTE: Some handlers like to give the dog a specific command that means to crawl through an object. This can make it easier to communicate to the dog from a distance that you want him to go through something instead of around, over or under it. You can use a command such as Crawl or Through.

GOAL: To teach the dog to go through narrow, low objects.

OBJECTIVE: To have the dog crawl through narrow openings and tunnels.

METHOD

Locate a culvert or other tunnel-like object that is safe—no more than 5 to 10 feet long and wide enough for your dog to walk through easily. An assistant goes to the other end with the dog and positions him so he sees you through the tunnel. When you have your dog's attention, call him. At the same time, the assistant encourages the dog to go through the tunnel. Praise him when he reaches you. Then send the dog back through the tunnel to the assistant. Use the go-to command if the dog has learned it.

PROBLEMS

Often a dog refuses to go through the tunnel or culvert. If this happens, find one that is shorter and wider and use until the dog goes through it. As the dog gains confidence, make the tunnel longer and smaller,

Handler Lisa Berry and her dog Zeke (Rottweiler) practicing a six-foot catwalk for Dogs East group.

Handler Teresa Dotson and her dog Zephyr (Border Collie) practicing agility training for Dogs East group.

Handler Joy Zerfing and her dog Boots (German Shepherd) training the Bark and Dig Alert to use in a disaster. Dogs East group.

Sharon Johnson and Brecon (Border Collie) practicing agility training for Dogs East group.

Rachel Yelle and Tally practicing a lift for disaster training. Photo courtesy of Bob Koenig.

Katie Schusler and Shadow practicing agility training. Photo courtesy of Bob Koenig.

Handler Bridgette Holder with her Bernese Mountain Dog practicing preliminary training for Directed Searching. Durham (NC) SAR

Handler Teresa MacPherson and Bama (Labrador Retriever) practicing the teeter-totter for disaster work. Dogs East group.

Handler Sharon Jones and Brecon (Border Collie) practicing agility training for Dogs East group.

but always easy for the dog to pass through. Be sure to give the dog plenty of praise for completing the exercise.

TEST

Use a tunnel about as tall as the dog is at his shoulders and about 10 feet long. Upon command, the dog walks through the tunnel to an assistant. The assistant sends the dog back through the tunnel to the handler. The dog passes through the tunnel confidently and without hesitation.

TRAVERSING SLICK AND UNSTABLE SURFACES

GOAL: To have the dog maneuver over slick and unstable surfaces with confidence.

OBJECTIVE: To teach the dog to spread his toes to gain control on slick, unstable surfaces.

METHOD

Use material such as a plastic tarp, wire mesh, plywood sheets, or whatever the dog is not used to walking on. Aluminum foil is good because of the strange noises created as the dog walks over it. This is especially true if the foil is placed on carpet or grass. Start with small pieces or sections of the material and allow the dog to walk over it on a flat area. As the dog's confidence increases, enlarge the surface and add a slope. As the dog feels himself sliding, he will naturally spread his toes to gain control. As he practices, he learns to spread his toes on slick surfaces.

TRAVERSING MOVING SURFACES
LEVEL 1: WALKING A BOARD

GOAL: To have the dog walk over a board four inches wide.

OBJECTIVE: To teach the dog not to jump off objects that move.

METHOD

Place a board, 12 inches wide and thick enough to support the weight of the dog without bouncing, on cinder blocks or bricks spaced about two feet apart. Encourage the dog to walk across the board. Be sure to let the dog examine the board if he wants, to help alleviate fear.

As the dog gains confidence, require him to walk over boards that become progressively narrower until you dog can walk a board four inches wide. Be sure to praise the dog when he walks the board.

Once the dog will walk on a narrow board, remove some support so it starts to bounce. Gradually remove more support so the board becomes unstable. The ultimate goal is to have the dog stop when the board bounces and then move slowly when told to. Use the commands wait and slow. He will soon learn to move slowly and stop. You can also practice the back command and get the dog used to moving back in similar situations.

PROBLEMS:

Initially, the dog will want to jump over the board or rush so fast he jumps off. Encourage the dog to walk the board by giving him a heel command and walking. If that doesn't work, have someone stand next to you with the dog between and walk him on the board. Encourage the dog to walk slowly and think about what he is doing.

TEST

With a board no wider than four inches and very springy (the amount of support to create a springy board will depend upon how thick the board is as well as the weight of the dog), the handler commands the dog to walk the board. The dog walks with control and confidence.

LEVEL 2: TEETER-TOTTER

GOAL: To teach the dog to walk on unsteady surfaces and also to use his weight to balance.

OBJECTIVE: To teach the dog to pause, balance and walk confidently when he senses unstable footing and surface movement.

METHOD

The dog must first learn to walk over a board so he is not worried by the narrowness of the teeter-totter. He is introduced to movement under his feet. Start him on the ground end of the teeter-totter, rather than in the middle. With the dog on leash, have him walk slowly up the teeter-totter. When he gets to the middle, give him a wait command and let him become aware of the sensation of the teeter-totter moving a little as he shifts his feet and weight. Allow the dog to balance in the middle of the teeter-totter to learn to keep it level by shifting his weight. While encouraging the dog, have him walk forward as the teeter-totter starts to descend. Once the dog reaches the other side and the teeter-totter has come to the ground again, praise him heartily and do it again. If the dog seems the least bit nervous, only perform this exercise two or three times a session until the dog is comfortable.

TEST

The handler gives the dog the command to walk over a teeter-totter starting at the end on the ground. When the dog reaches the middle, he balances the teeter-totter until instructed to go forward. The dog goes forward until the teeter-totter reaches the ground.

LEVEL 3: ADVANCED TEETER-TOTTER

GOAL: To have the dog walk a teeter-totter that is moving in both directions.

OBJECTIVE: To teach the dog to handle an object that moves more than on way at a time.

Method

Place the teeter-totter or a board on a small barrel. At first, allow the dog to walk the teeter-totter without the barrel moving. When he is comfortable with this, move the barrel slightly. This can be accomplished in a number of ways. A rope or long pipe can be passed through the barrel with a handler holding each end to move the barrel alone without the board. The dog should be able to wait, back, and turn around while on the board, teeter-totter or barrel.

TEST

The handler commands the dog to start to walk up a teeter-totter on a barrel. An assistant moves the barrel while the dog walks the teeter-totter. When the dog reaches the center and balances, the handler tells the dog to wait, turn around and then lets the dog walk back down the teeter-totter until he is on the ground.

CLOSED-END TUNNEL

GOAL: To send the dog into a closed-end tunnel, go up and return.

OBJECTIVE: To enable the dog to search in areas that are small and dark.

METHOD

The plastic or cloth tunnels used in agility trials are ideal for this lesson. They are open at one end and lay flat and closed on the other. You can make one using any material, such as plastic or canvas. Fold the material in half and sew it together down the side. It should be at least six feet long. Next, attach one end around a hula hoop and allow the opposite end to lie flat. Once the tunnel is secure, with the hula hoop forming an opening to your man-made cave, send the dog through. You may have to open the other end at first to get the dog to pass through. Gradually, close the opening until the dog will go through the tunnel with the other end lying flat. Once the dog does this readily, use a culvert or pipe of some kind, about two feet in diameter, with one end blocked. Send the dog into the closed-end tunnel on a search or look command. Be sure to place something to find in the tunnel occasionally, so the dog has the reward of finding an object. Remember to praise the dog when he returns to you.

TEST

Use a culvert that is no shorter than the dog's shoulders and has been blocked off at one end. The culvert should be at least three times longer than the dog's length from nose to tail tip. The handler sends the dog into the culvert. The dog enters the culvert with enthusiasm and shows no fear or hesitation.

THE HOLD-IT COMMAND

GOAL: To teach the dog to hold an object in his mouth.

OBJECTIVE: To have the dog hold an article in his mouth after he has been told to take it.

METHOD

Once the dog is willing to take an object in his mouth, start the Hold-It command. First, get the dog to take the object in his mouth. Then, very gently, touch the bottom of his jaw and tell him to Hold It. Be careful not to press his jaw closed in a way that might hurt him or make him feel uncomfortable. If you do, the dog will want to spit the article out right away. If the dog holds the article loosely, gently wiggle the article. Most dogs will automatically clamp down. Praise him if he does. Have the dog hold the article only for a few seconds at first and gradually build up the length of time he holds it.

When the dog is willing to hold the article, have him walk with it. If he drops it as he starts to walk, give him the take-it command, tell him to Hold It and start over.

TEST

The handler commands the dog to take an article, either from his hand or from the ground. After the dog has the article, the handler will tell him to Hold It. The dog holds the article firmly for at least 30 seconds.

THE OUT COMMAND

GOAL: To have the dog release an object (including food).

OBJECTIVE: To teach the dog to release immediately on command anything he has in his mouth.

METHOD

Start this exercise using food. Once the dog learns to release food, he will release anything in his mouth. Food is the hardest yet the most important object to get a dog to spit out. Things he picks up and wants to eat may cause harm. Begin with food that has substance and is not messy, such as a dog biscuit or hard cheese. Use a piece small enough to fit between your thumb and index finger. Put the dog in a sitting position in front and facing you. Place the food between your fingers and extend your hand toward the dog. As soon as the dog opens his mouth to take the food, put your fingers in his mouth. He will close his mouth on your fingers (the first time may be a little rough, but you should not be bitten), and when he realizes it is your finger, he will open his mouth. As soon as you feel his mouth on your fingers, give the Out command. When his mouth opens, pull your fingers out and praise him, giving him the food immediately.

Only do this exercise a few times in a session. Once the dog gets the idea, he will go along with it. When he understands the exercise, extend the food beyond your fingers, so he feels the food in his mouth; repeat the same procedure, giving the Out command. Work to where you give him the food and he spits it out on command.

Next, use nonfood items, giving the food reward as soon as the dog spits the item out. Gradually eliminate he food from the exercise.

TEST

The handler puts a piece of hard food, such as a dog biscuit, on the ground and tells the dog to take it. When the dog has the biscuit in his mouth, the handler gives the Out command. The dog spits the biscuit out. When he does this, the handler tells the dog okay and lets him eat the biscuit. The handler then gives the dog an object, tells the dog to take it and then Out, and then praises the dog.

THE FETCH COMMAND

GOAL: To have the dog retrieve an article.

OBJECTIVE: To teach the dog to put the Go, Take It, Hold It, Come and Out commands into a retrieve routine.

METHOD

This exercise teaches the dog a pattern of behavior, or a routine. Work on leash until you feel you have total control over the dog.

Pick an object or article the dog likes, such as a toy, ball or stick. Be sure the object is not uncomfortable or difficult for the dog to handle and hold in his mouth. Get the dog excited by teasing with the article as you did in the take-it exercise. Toss the article a short distance, and encourage the dog to go and get it as you give the Fetch command. When he reaches the article tell him to take it, hold it, and then call him back to you. It may be necessary to coax him by gently pulling on his leash. Once the dog reaches you, give him the sit and out commands. Repeat this exercise until the dog understands that Fetch means to go find the article, pick it up and bring it to you.

TEST

The dog starts at heel position. The handler tosses an object about 20 feet away. The handler commands the dog to go to the object, take it up, hold it and bring it back. This can be done with individual commands or with the Fetch command.

The Jumping Command

GOAL: To teach the dog to judge his jump to be able to clear an obstacle with minimal effort.

OBJECTIVE: To help the dog gain confidence in jumping

METHOD

There is more to jumping than doing it on command. Do choose a specific command for jumping. Teaching the dog how to judge his jump requires a specific technique. One method that is very successful is the Clothier Natural Jumping Method. This method is based on training horses. While this method stresses a showy jumping style for obedience, it does teach the dog how to handle different types of jumps or varying widths, heights, shapes and distances, which is a useful skill for the SAR dog.

The Clothier Method emphasizes measuring the dog's height and, using a formula, placing jumps to allow the dog to jump within his stride. By changing distances and allowing the dog to experience different strides between jumps, you teach the dog how to judge the jump. This results in an easy rhythm of jumping that is pleasant, low stress, and carefully controlled.

In teaching, avoid asking the dog to jump obstacles that force him to stumble, strain and experience stress. While in a real search situation, you cannot control the distance the dog must jump. Teaching him in a way that builds confidence will allow him to handle the search with more control.

If you do not wish to follow the Clothier Method, start your dog with low, single jumps. Minimize any jumping exercises for young dogs of breeds especially prone to hip dysplasia or elbow problems. However, low, easy jumps can be used to teach the dog the Jump command.

Walk the dog up to the jump and let him look at it until his curiosity is satisfied. Next, encourage the dog to jump over, giving a command, such as Jump, Over, or Hup. If the dog seems confused, walk over the jump with the dog to show him. Praise the dog as soon as he goes over the jump with you. As the dog gets the idea, stand next to the jump, point toward the jump and give the Jump command. When he clears the jump, encourage him to return by jumping back. Once the dog is physically able to handle it, increase the height and width of the jump and set up a series of jumps. Be sure they are placed far enough apart to allow the dog enough time and stride to jump comfortably. Again, you are not looking for speed and flash, but rather a well-controlled jump.

TEST

With two jumps set at a height and width suitable for the size and age of the dog, the handler gives the dog the command to Jump. The dog jumps with ease and enthusiasm.

The Speak Command

GOAL: The dog will learn to bark on command.

OBJECTIVE: To teach the dog to bark on command in order to use the bark as an alert.

METHOD 1

There are a number of ways to teach a dog to speak. The most successful way is to use food and tease the dog until he becomes so frustrated he barks. Hold the food just out of reach of the dog and pull it away as he grabs for it. As you tease, give the dog the command to Speak and get him excited. Once the dog barks, immediately give him the food and praise, saying, "Good Speak!" It usually takes once or twice for the dog to make the connection.

METHOD 2

Some dogs have been taught so well to be quiet that they have a hard time understanding that they are now being asked to bark. Set up a situation in which you know the dog will bark naturally, such as when the doorbell rings or someone knocks on the door. Arrange for this to happen and, just before the event occurs, give the dog the Speak command. When the dog barks, give him the treat and praise. Repeat this until the dog makes the connection.

TEST

The handler sits the dog and gives the dog the Speak command. The dog barks with control.

THE QUIET COMMAND

GOAL: To teach the dog he must be quiet on command.

OBJECTIVE: The dog learns to stop making noise when told.

METHOD

Once the dog knows how to speak on command, you can teach him to be quiet on command. This is best taught when the dog is barking on a speak command and not barking at something else. Put the dog in a sit-stay and give him the speak command. As soon as the dog has barked a few times, tell him Quiet and touch his mouth with a treat in your hand. Let him sniff the treat to get him to stop barking. When he stops barking, give him a treat. Repeat this command until the dog understands and stops barking on command.

TEST

The handler puts the dog in a sit-stay, gives the speak command and then after a few barks gives the Quiet command. The dog stops barking within one bark and remains quiet.

ARTICLE

For certain aspects of search work, some people want their dogs to retrieve an article. The retrieved article is a form of an alert similar to a bringsel. Some handlers teach the dog to pick up a stick or whatever the dog may find near a victim and bring it back as an alert. However, when an article is considered evidence, it is not a good idea to have the dog touch anything. The police may want to send the article to the lab for analysis and will not want dog saliva on it. Also, the position and location of an article is often important. In the wilderness, an article verified as belonging to a victim can mean a shift in the Point Last Seen (PLS) and the search effort. Therefore, it is important to leave the article where it is. If an airscenting dog finds the article and leaves it untouched, a tracking dog can be scented on the article to track a victim.

Those of you who want to teach your dogs to pick up a stick or whatever is available near a victim and bring it back as a for of alert (or to use the bringsel alert) may need to teach your dogs to retrieve. A word of caution: If the dog does not have a natural desire to retrieve, many SAR handlers feel the dog will not make a good search dog. If your dog does like to retrieve, refine his retrieve to make it reliable.

BUILDING THE DESIRE TO RETRIEVE

GOAL: To have the dog chase a play object.

OBJECTIVE: To enhance the dog's retrieve desire.

METHOD

Let the dog sniff and bite the retrieve object. A ball works very well. Once you have the dog's attention, roll the ball away from the dog. If he shows no interest, tease the dog with the ball. Be sure to encourage the dog and get him excited. As soon as the dog takes the ball in his mouth, praise him as you give him a command to take the ball: Take it, good boy, take it! Once the dog is excited, roll the ball away from the dog. As he chases the ball, give him a command to get the ball. Praise him as he gets it. Be sure to do all work on-leash so you can call the dog back and encourage him to bring the ball to you.

PROBLEMS

Some dogs just do not seem to want to retrieve an object. They will chase the object and not pick it up, grab the object and refuse to come back, or refuse to release it when they do return. If this happens, you must break the exercise into its smallest components and teach the dog each step. Teach the dog in the following order: seek or find it; take it; hold it; out; fetch.

Once the dog knows all these commands, be sure not to use your command to find evidence when sending the dog to retrieve an object for you.

Some handlers think it is necessary to use a modified force-retrieve method to teach their dogs. It is not a good idea to use this method because a dog who does not have a natural desire to retrieve may not make a good SAR dog. A dog who is not motivated to retrieve should not be forced to retrieve as an alert because the reliability of the alert will be questionable. The alert should be something the dog does naturally and enjoys since he must give you his alert when he is very tired.

TEST

The handler teases the dog with an object, such as a ball or toy, tossing the object upwind about 20 feet away, and gives the command Fetch. The dog brings the object back to the handler.

Riva training for dead scent using the "daisy wheel."

Chapter 18
Additional Problems

Game Chasing

Game chasing can develop any time in a dog's life—causing a frustrating problem for SAR dog handlers. The ideas presented here should help prevent and break a dog from game chasing and can be applied to other similar problems.

The following three methods sometimes used to break dogs from chasing game are not recommended:

1. The first requires the assistance of a veterinarian and involves injecting a dog with a substance such as lithium chloride just before allowing the dog to chase game. The dog may become so sick he will feel as though he is dying. Theoretically, the dog will associate the sickness with the game or the scent of game and not chase game again.
2. The second method uses an electronic shock collar.
3. The third involves attaching a dead animal or part of it to the dog's collar until it rots off.

These methods have questionable results and may cause more problems than they cure. This is especially true if the first and second methods mentioned are not done properly. Question the reliability of a dog's use in SAR if such drastic measures must be used to cure him of game chasing.

Overview

Before you can successfully use the following methods to break a dog of game chasing, review the chapter, "Concepts of Dog Training." When working with your dog, a head harness, such as the *Easy Walker* or *HALTI,* is much better than a choke collar or a buckle collar. The head harness fits over the dog's head and attaches under the dog's chin, and functions in much the same manner as a hackamore halter on a horse. This enables the handler to divert the dog's head away from the object to be avoided and focus on an acceptable object—and is accomplished without harsh leash-jerk techniques. The head harness allows the handler to control his dog with less effort. If the dog is not obedience trained to the off-leash level, start obedience training at the same time as you start working on the game-chasing problem. However, do not do both in the same training session.

The first question to consider when dealing with a dog who chases game is whether he has been trained to chase other animals or has a naturally strong chase tendency. A dog may be trained to chase squirrels, rabbits, cats, etc. for fun by family members. If this is the case, it makes the habit much more difficult, and sometimes impossible, to cure. If the dog has not been trained to chase a specific type of animal, but has a strong prey-chase instinct (such as the herding breeds), then you must try to redirect that instinct toward finding people instead of game.

The methods suggested in this book can be applied to dogs of all ages, although prevention with a puppy is much easier and more effective than trying to cure a dog who is a seasoned game chaser. As a rule, the longer a dog has been chasing game, the longer and more difficult it will be to cure him. If you find the techniques do not seem to bring even a slight improvement after a reasonable amount of time (about two weeks), break the training into smaller, less complicated tasks. Frequently, a dog fails to respond because he cannot comprehend so much at once. By breaking the training into smaller tasks, you allow the dog and yourself to make progress. If you still do not have success, combine both of the desensitizing techniques mentioned in this chapter.

To break a dog of game chasing, you must change a behavior or habit. There are three things you must do to change the habit: desensitize the dog to the game; gain control over the dog; and reward him for an alternate habit replacing the old behavior. Since game chasing is a highly "charged" or "rewarding" habit, it takes persistence to change. (Consider how hard it is to break your own habits).

The training sessions should occur regularly. Train at least three times a week but not more than three times daily. Do all of your work on-leash until you are 99 percent sure your dog is cured. As a rule, it takes about six weeks to change a behavior. It is absolutely necessary during the training six-week period that the dog lacks the opportunity to chase game.

Prevention

To prevent an older dog or a puppy from developing an interest in game chasing, focus on control techniques and direct his prey-chase instinct toward finding humans. If dealing with a puppy, the best time to do this is before he is six months old. At this time in a puppy's life, it is natural for him to follow and learn from his mother or leader (in this case, you). If you have another dog who is trained and not a game chaser, allow the puppy to walk in the woods with both of you and associate-learn from the older dog. Each time the dogs come across game, respond by calling them to you. Use positive training techniques. Harsh methods will not create the bond you need for SAR work. When a puppy is very young (six to twelve weeks), you can praise him for what he does right in your daily interaction with him. No formal training is done at this time. Most young puppies are not very brave or confident. At this time, introduce a puppy to game and call him to you, away from the game. Praise him as he sits by you to teach him to avoid game. As he gets older and gains confidence, he will not be frightened by game or have the desire to chase game.

For those brave puppies who do not run from game at a very young age, call the puppy to you with gentle guidance from the leash if necessary. Praise him when he turns away from the game and comes in your direction. Be sure to make a big fuss when he reaches you.

While the puppy is young, do not allow anyone to encourage him to chase any type of animal. From a very young age introduce the pup to other animals, with control. If you proof him as a youngster, he will not be interested in game when he is older. Only allow him to chase nonliving things, such as balls, sticks, etc. and only as a game with you.

After six months, the puppy's tendency to follow diminishes as he becomes interested in exploring and putting to use what he has learned. Therefore, it is important to establish yourself as his leader before he is six months of age. Keep in mind, a dog can go through one or two periods of rebellion. The first period usually occurs when the dog is nine to twelve months old. The second may occur when the dog is around 18 months. If your dog tests your leadership during these periods, it is important to maintain your control.

Method I

To desensitize your dog to game, it is important to expose him to game gradually. You can start with some commercial scents available to train dogs to hunt or with deer hooves from hunters. Use the commercial scent on a rag or the hoof, which is tied to a string and left in a visible place outside. Work your dog at a heel, or on a free leash (where he is allowed to walk the full length of the leash but not allowed to pull). Start downwind, near the scented rag, and move toward the rag. The instant the dog shows any interest in the scented rag, walk in the opposite direction, telling the dog to heel. Praise him as he ignores the scent. Do not give him a jerk on the leash for looking at the scented rag or acknowledge the presence of the scent yourself. The idea is to show disinterest in the scent; show by example that it is something to walk away from. When he ignores the scent reliably, you are ready for the next step.

First, have someone stand about 50 feet away from the scented rag attached to a string held by an out-of-sight assistant. As you approach the scented rag, the helper slowly moves the scented rag away from the dog. As your dog notices the rag moving, follow the same procedure as you did when the rag was still. Work to where your dog ignores the rag when it is rapidly jerking. Practice this exercise in different locations and in environments in which the dog will most likely encounter game. Again, when you reach the point where your dog makes no move toward the scented rag (he is allowed a disinterested look at most), you are ready for the next step.

When you have mastered the scented rag, you are ready to train using wild animals or domesticated livestock. Use game the dog likes to chase. Start tempting your dog with either the game he likes or an animal in a cage. If this is not possible, use a cat, chickens, etc., in an area within sight of the dog, but not accessible to him. Repeat the process as above until the dog shows, at most, a disinterested look in the direction of the animal. Continue this process with wild game such as squirrels, which are readily available in most areas, until you can walk in the woods without the dog chasing game.

For dogs who chase large game such as deer, it is a good idea to start with small animals to gain control and work up to large animals. Since it is not easy to find tame deer, you may have to walk in the woods to try to flush some out. If you cannot get a supply of game to use, try to gain permission to work near a farm, zoo, horseback riding academy, or some place that has livestock or animals. People who train hunting dogs usually have a supply of game available for their training needs. Hanging the rear legs of deer about 10-15 yards away from your victim is another method you can use to desensitize your dog to game. Be sure to keep your dog on-leash until he shows no interest in the deer. If necessary, start your desensitization technique with deer droppings.

Method II

If you try Method I and you find after a few weeks that your dog does not calm down and become disinterested in the scented rag or the actual game, include a diversionary tactic initiated the instant the dog shows interest in the rag or the game. The positive tactic, such as a play session, a favorite toy, or favorite food, etc. is to divert the dog's attention and interest from the scent to you. To succeed, the dog must want the diversion more than the prey. Use very special foods, games or objects, given only during this diversion training. Occasionally, you must develop the dog's desire for the diversion before the training session. The scenario is the same as Method I, except that, at the point where the dog shows interest in the scented rag or game, you initiate the diversionary technique. Be sure to keep up the diversion until the dog relaxes and shows no interest in the scented rag or the game. At this point, you can heel the dog away from the game.

Control Techniques

For those dogs who are older or are persistent game chasers, further develop your control over the dog. To do this you should use a number of passive techniques. Aggressive techniques usually involve physical abuse of the dog. While aggressive techniques will work, they do not produce a reliable performance from a dog. The dog responds primarily out of fear instead of a desire to please.

Remember, to establish your leadership and your dog's role of follower, you must use movement. Eliminate all cases in which your dog dictates the activity between you. For example, don't allow him to come over and nudge your hand or arm to be petted. He controls your behavior by dictating what you are to do (pet him). It is important for all free fondling and petting of your dog to stop. If your dog comes over to you and demands to be petted, you must make him earn it by doing something simple, such as Sit. Then, give him a pat or two, but don't go overboard. His main interaction and reward from you will be when he gets praise and attention for not chasing game.

It is important to withhold all extra treats for at least six weeks. After six weeks, be sure he earns his one treat a day. Do not allow your dog to go before you through doors, etc. The dog should not have more than one toy during the six weeks of training. Do not play any tug-of-war games. Do not yell at your dog, but instead use a quiet, firm voice. Make your dog do a long (15 to 20 minutes) Down once a day. Pull surprise Downs randomly at least once a week. Do not allow your dog to sleep on the bed with you. It is okay for your dog to sleep in the bedroom, which promotes positive bonding, but not on the bed. Have two obedience sessions a day with exercises the dog knows. If the dog is not obedience trained, be sure to have at least one five-minute session a day to teach obedience, and one practice for only the things he already knows. These should be at least three hours apart.

Part of the reward of game chasing is the release of built up energy; therefore, it is critical for the dog to get plenty of exercise. Each dog requires a different amount of exercise; you have exercised your dog enough if he wants to rest upon returning home. The dog who goes out for a one-mile jog with his owner and comes back full of energy has just been given a warm-up. Some very high energy dogs may need two exercise sessions a day.

Conclusion

To prevent a dog from becoming a game chaser, establish a strong bond between you and your dog, prove yourself the leader, and set the rules. When working with a game chaser, do not be discouraged if these methods do not work right away. The longer a dog has been game chasing, the longer it will take you to retrain him. Be inventive, but be honest with yourself. No matter how good your SAR dog may be, his worth is questionable if he is a chronic or persistent game chaser. If you cannot trust him 100 percent, perhaps you should consider using another dog.

Burnout

Some dogs seem to suffer burnout. This shows up in the SAR dog when the dog who has been working well suddenly loses interest in part or all of the SAR work. There are many ways to deal with this problem. First, review the methods you used to train and maintain your dog. If your dog has learned his lessons well, is performing well, and you have switched your maintenance techniques to short problems to keep him interested, give him a long, tough problem. Dogs do get bored with the work. If you have been doing all long, tough problems, do some short ones.

Another cause of burnout is familiarity with the training area. While dogs may not think and reason as we do, they do have a tremendous power of recall. It is not unusual for a dog to remember an area he worked over a year ago.

A dog may perform poorly because of familiarity with the victim. A dog does not forget the scent of people he has met even a few times. Finding new victims to train with is one of the most difficult aspects of SAR dog work. Because of this, many SAR units have to use the same people repeatedly. When a dog is given a choice of two tracks or scents, some dogs will go for the scent of the stranger instead of the scent of a friend. After using the same person as a victim many times, some dogs do not show enthusiasm for finding the people they know.

Seasoned SAR dogs do not always take training seriously. They do know the difference between a real search and a mock search. Another trick to spark a dog's interest in SAR work again is to send him out on a search training session with no victim in his area. Intermittent reinforcement is the strongest type of reinforcement, and it will enhance the dog's performance to find no victim once in awhile.

Sometimes the dog just needs a vacation from the work. If the dog does not pick up after a few weeks, and seems to have a continued loss of interest in SAR work, have him checked out by a veterinarian to be sure he is healthy. If age and physical problems are ruled out, then you may have to give him a few months off. When you begin again, work back up through the levels of training rather than starting where you left off.

The key factor in retraining the dog should be your enthusiasm for the work. The dog will not forget what he has been previously taught. It is very difficult for some people to understand or accept the fact that dogs, like people, change as they grow older. If your dog still shows a lack of interest or an unreliable performance level, then you may have to face the fact he is no longer useful as an SAR dog.

Chapter 19
The Rewards of Canine Search and Rescue

Over the years, I have spoken with many people who are involved in search and rescue work, both with and without dogs. While everyone has personal reasons for getting involved, there seems to be a common thread among most of the personnel involved. People enjoy helping other people. They enjoy using their skills or hobby to do a "real" job. For example, the diver enjoys his sport but wants to take it a step further; the veteran medic wants to share his skills and abilities with the community; or the canine handler loves his dog and wants to do something meaningful. All agree that the rewards are worth the personal expense, time and effort it takes to become part of a professional volunteer organization. In some cases, people are employed by the rescue unit. And for many of those people, this is the ultimate situation: being paid to do the job they love.

People enjoy search work because it is like solving a mystery. They rise to the urgency and excitement of search missions. They relish the sense of belonging and experiencing unity among rescue people, regardless of position in life, race, religion, or geographic location. They thrive on it because of the teamwork required to run a mission as well as to search through the field. They love just being outdoors.

There is a lighter side to canine search work as well. You are often asked to give talks and demonstrations to children. On one occasion, I gave a talk to a state police camp for young adults. After my brief speech, I was asked to give a demonstration. One youngster laid a track and the dog followed it to find him. Next, a trooper had an unusual request. It seems that the rules of the camp required that the young adults were to put away all of their clothing. Well, one boy had left a pair of underwear in the showers. No one would come forward and claim the underwear in public. So the trooper asked if my dog could identify the person who owned the underwear. I told him I'd be glad to try.

Much to the amusement of the girls, we had the boys form two lines, one arm's length apart. Next, I scented the dog on the underwear and started down the line. I had all I could do to keep a straight face because with every boy I passed, I heard loud sighs of "Whew!" and "Oh, boy." As we got closer and closer to the cabins, the dog indicated that the scent was in one of them. (It turned out that the "guilty" boy slept in that cabin.) Next, he worked down the second line, but gave no immediate indication of which boy was the owner of the underwear. We passed back down the line and the dog stopped in front of one boy. You can imagine the hoopin' and hollerin' that took place when it was confirmed that we had found the owner of the underwear! Later the trooper told me that as soon as we started down the first line the boy confessed—dogs usually have that effect on those who are guilty.

As far as the dog goes, I could have sworn I saw a gleam of mischief in his eyes. It is amazing to watch my own skilled dog work with me as a team member. Training a "regular" pet to be a search dog produces a total metamorphosis in behavior and attitude. The dog knows just what to do and does not need to be told. The bond that develops as you work with your dog on numerous missions is deeper than any other. The rewards of Canine Search and Rescue are enormous.

PART IV
RESOURCE MATERIAL

Appendix A
TRAINING OUTLINE

Suggested below are outlines listing in order the phases of training for each operational level of SAR dog work. Wilderness training (airscenting and scent discrimination) provides a solid foundation and a good place to start for all other types of SAR dog work. This is where the dog learns the concept that he must find a human.

Airscenting Dog

Wilderness
1. Teach the Mechanics of the Alert
2. Start Obedience
3. Beginner Runaway
4. Novice Runaway
5. Intermediate Runaway
6. Advanced Runaway
7. Beginning Re-find
8. Alert
9. Advanced Re-find
10. Trail Problem
11. Beginning Area Problem
12. Advanced Area Problem
13. Beginning Night Problem
14. Advanced Night Problem
15. Heavy Brush Problem
16. Multiple Victim Problem
17. Beginning Moving Victim Problem
18. Intermediate Moving Victim Problem
19. Advanced Moving Victim
20. More Advanced Moving Victim

Scent Discriminatory Dog

Wilderness
1. Teach the Mechanics of the Alert
2. Start Obedience
3. Runaway
4. Scent Article-Runaway
5. Identification
6. Tougher Trail Problem
7. No Scent Article
8. Aged Trail
9. More Complicated Trails

10. Contaminated Trail
11. Unknown Person
12. ID From A Group
13. Contaminated Scent Article
14. Tougher Contaminated Scent Problem

Water Search Training

Airscenting and Tracking/Trailing Dog
1. Qualified in Wilderness Training
2. Preparation for Water Training
3. Beginning Water Training
4. Working From the Shore
5. Multiple Boats

Evidence Search

Airscenting and Tracking/Trailing Dog
1. Qualified in Wilderness Training
2. Mechanics of the Alert
3. Beginning Article
4. Hidden Article

Small-Area or Fine-Search Techniques

Airscenting and Tracking/Trailing Dog
1. Qualified in Wilderness Training
2. Evidence Search (No Retrieve)
3. Fine Search Technique

Cadaver Training

Airscenting and Tracking/Trailing Dog
1. Qualified in Wilderness Training
2. Small Area or Fine Search Techniques
3. Underground Victim
4. Above Ground Hidden Cadaver

Avalanche Training

Airscenting and Tracking/Trailing Dog
1. Qualified in Wilderness Training
2. Preparing for Avalanche Training
3. Finding A Victim

Disaster Training

Airscenting and Tracking/Trailing Dog
1.   Qualified in Wilderness Training
2.   Additional Commands
3.   Buried Victim
4.   Bodies Only
5.   Advanced Disaster Work

Article
1.   Obedience
2.   Building The Desire to Retrieve
3.   Intermediate Retrieve
4.   Advanced Article Search

Appendix B
SAR Dog Handler Training

Because different regions of the country have different terrain features and weather conditions, the training necessary to function safely in a search situation varies widely. Listed below are some of the types of additional training a person may need to be a qualified search and rescue dog handler. In some cases, understanding different search techniques will help you assist agencies or units which specialize in these types of rescue missions or at least to know when to call the agencies that offer the rescue expertise needed to handle the situation.

If you are not sure what is necessary for your region, consult established rescue units such as local park rangers, departments of environmental resources personnel, military establishments, law enforcement agencies, fire departments, dive squads, forest rangers, sheriff's department, etc.

I recommend that the SAR dog handler receive, at minimum, certification in the topics preceded with an "*."

Hazardous Materials Training (HAZMET)
*First Aid—Minimum Red Cross First Aid training including CPR
*Managing the Search Operation or Managing the Search Function
*Mantracking
Emergency Medical Technician
Wilderness Medical Training
*Orienteering
Urban Medicine
Wilderness Survival
Avalanche Survival Training
*Unstable Structure Awareness
Heavy Rescue
*Water Self-Rescue
High Angle Rescue
Confined Space Rescue
*Canine First Aid
Ocean Rescue Techniques
Swift Water Rescue
Beach and Surf Rescue
*Management of Spontaneous Volunteers
Trauma of the Elderly
Pediatric Trauma
Trauma Care in the Field
*Helicopter Operations for SAR

In-Water Helicopter Rescue
Canine Rope Rescue Techniques
Critical Incident Stress Management
Infrared Resources
Nutrition and Fluid Replacement for SAR
*Personal Preparedness for SAR
Resource Status Display System
Field Electronic Navigation Techniques
Geographic Information Systems for Emergency Response
Urban SAR Problems
Mountain Rescue Techniques and Survival
Desert Survival

Below are various publications and organizations of interest to the SAR dog handler, as well as a complete list of all the canine units for the United States and Canada. Because of the skills and teamwork necessary to be a successful SAR dog handler, it is futile to train on your own. Join an established SAR Dog Unit. It is also much more difficult to gain recognition by established rescue and law enforcement agencies as an independent. Remember, someone's life depends on you and your dog.

RESPONSE *Magazine*
The Journal of Search, Rescue and Emergency Response
P.O. Box 3709
Fairfax VA 22038
703/352-1349

(A subscription to *RESPONSE* is included with membership in the National Association for Search and Rescue, NASAR).

NASAR
PO Box 3709
Fairfax VA 22038

RESCUE *Magazine*
PO Box 27966
San Diego CA 92128
800/334-8152

SAR Dog ALERT
3310 Wren Lane
Eagan MN 55121-2324
612/452-4209

For a list of suppliers for SAR dog equipment and other canine related organizations consult *ALMOST EVERYTHING YOU ALWAYS WANTED TO KNOW ABOUT DOGS, THE CANINE SOURCE BOOK*, by Susan Bulanda, (Fourth Edition) published by Doral Publishing.

Appendix C
Search and Rescue Units

CANADA

Canadian SAR Dogs
Bill Grimmer
PO Box 126
993 Scoudouc Rd
Scoudouc NB E0A 1N0
Information 506/ 532-4988
Call Out 506/ 532-6691

Central NOVA Man-Trailers
Darrell Mills
RR 2
Stewiak NS B0N 2I0
Information & Call Out 902/ 673-2987
 or 455-4647

New Brunswick Ground SAR Assoc
Box 536
Hartland NB E0J 1N0

Nova Scotia Ground SAR Assoc
W L McLaughlin
PO Box 1502
Halifax NS B3J 2Y3

Provincial Emergency Program
Erin Wilson
7464 149-A
Surrey BC V3S 3H6
Information 604/ 597-6182

Sauvetage Canada Rescue
Art Galarneau
PO Box 145
Pierrefonds QUE H9H 4K0
Information 514/ 434-2735
Call Out 514/ 331-6100 X 4872

SAR Dog Assoc of Alberta
Kevin George
7120 91st
Edmonton AB T6E 2Z7
Information 403/ 469-6509
Call Out 800/ 272-9600

Timmins SAR
RR #2 Kraft Creek Rd
Timmins ONT P4N 7C3
West NOVA SAR Dog Assoc
Susan Tabor
PO Box 70
Cambridge Station NS B0P 1G0
Information 902/ 538-7919
Call Out 902/ 538-7919

UNITED STATES NATIONAL UNITS

International Mantrailing Bloodhound Network
Bill Butler
31951 Lodgepole Dr
Evergreen CO 80439
Information 303/ 674-8317

International Rescue Dog Org
Caroline Hebard
104 Ballantine Rd
Bernardsville NJ 07924
908/766-7125

National Police Bloodhound Assoc
Becky Shaffer
PO Box 43
Dewart PA 17730

North American Search Dog Network
Joyce Phares
RR 2 Box 32
Urbana IL 61801
Information 217/ 367-5752

SAR Dogs of the United States, Inc
PO Box 11411
Denver CO 80211

SAR K-9 Service
PO Box 32621
Fridley MN 55432

ALASKA

Alaska SAR Dogs
Bill Tai
200 W 34th Ave # 665
Anchorage AK 99503
Information 907/ 344-7436
Call Out 907/ 269-5711

PAWS
Cathie Harms
PO Box 84388
Fairbanks AK 99708
Information 907/ 457-8210
Call Out 907/ 479-2016
or 907/ 452- 9256

SEADOGS
Bruce Bowler
PO Box 244
Juneau AK 99802
Information 907/ 465-2985
or 789-2582
Call Out 907/ 789-2161

Search Dogs Valdez
Box 2552
Valdez AK 99686

Sitka Volunteer Fire Dept
Rescue K-9's
Susan Royce
209 Lake St
Sitka AK 99835
Information 907/ 747-6064
Call Out 907/ 747-3233

ARIZONA

Cochise County Sheriff
SAR Dog Unit #1
Richard Chenlfant

NCR Box 335 c
Pierce AZ 85625
Information 602/ 824-3653
Call Out 800/ 362-0812

ARKANSAS

Arkansas SAR Dog Team
Tanya Cross
RT 3 Box 207
Lonoke AR 72036
Information 501/ 676-5078
Call Out 501/ 988-5141

Benton County SAR
David Comstock
12784 WC 28
Prairie Grove AR 72753
Information 501/ 846-2314
Call Out 501/ 271-1004

CALIFORNIA

Bay Area Rescue K-9
Linda Spangler
2211 Westchester Dr
San Jose CA 95124
Information 408/ 356-6519
Call Out 408/ 356-6519

Calif-Swiss Search Dog Assoc
Willy Grundherr
PO Box 66262
Scotts Valley CA 95066
Information 408/ 425-7661
Call Out 805/ 324-6551

California Rescue Dog Assoc
Shirley Hammond
1062 Metro Circle
Palo Alto CA 94303
Information 415/ 856-9669
Call Out 916/ 988-5542
or 916/ 989-4989

Contra Costa County Bloodhounds
Judy Robb
421 La Vista Rd
Walnut Creek CA 94598
Information 415/ 939-9279

Call Out 415/ 646-2441
 Los Angeles Search Dogs
Jerry Newcomb
3224 N Mount Curve
Altadena CA 91001
Information 818/ 798-7616
Call Out 213/ 264-7084

Orange County Sheriff's
SAR Reserve
Larry Harris
1807 Highland Dr
Newport Beach CA 92660
Information 714/ 665-1612
Call Out 714/ 647-1850

Sierra Madre SAR Team
Arnold Gaffrey
9527 Wedgewood
Temple City CA 91780
Information 818/ 286-8053 or 355-8000
Call Out 818/ 355-1414

WOOF Search Dogs
Marin County Sheriff's Dept
Civic Center
San Rafael CA 94903
Information 415/ 499-7243
Call Out 415/ 499-7243

COLORADO

Black Paws Search, Rescue
& Avalanche Dogs
Marie Cloughesy
13050 Black Forest Rd
Colorado Springs CO 80908
Information 719/ 495-3287
Call Out 800/ 851-3051

Front Range Rescue Dogs
Ann Wichmann
417 Sherman
Longmont CO 80501
Information 303/ 441-3408
or 776-3957
Call Out 303/ 441-4444

Larimer County SAR
and SAR Dogs of Colorado
Fran Lieser
4216 Glade Rd
Loveland CO 80537
Information 303/ 667-9931
Call Out 303/ 221-7141

Moffat County SAR K-9 Unit
Dennis Craig
221 W Victory Way
Craig CO 81625
Information 303/ 824-4495
Call Out 303/ 824-4495

United Search Dogs
Dixie Ferrick
26061 Co Rd H
Cortez CO 81321
Information 303/ 565-4593
Call Out 303/ 565-8441

CONNECTICUT

Connecticut State Police
Tpr K Rodino
Hartford Rd
Colchester CT 06415
Information 203/ 238-6026
Call Out 203/ 566-4240

Stafford PD
Lewis Fletcher
22 Chruch St
Stafford Springs CT 06076
Information & Call Out 203/ 684-4926

FLORIDA

Central Florida SAR Team
Carolyn Wheelis
PO Box 875
Eustis FL 32727-0875

ESAR/PAC
[Special Response Team]
Mike Turner
2923 Whirlaway
Tall FL 32308

Information 904/ 386-8850
Call Out 904/ 576-2709

FASTER K-9 Division
Lucy Walburn
PO Box 727
Chiefland FL 32626-0727
Information 904/ 493-0282
or 493-6181
Call Out 800/ 945-3278

Florida Disaster Dog
Search Team, Inc
Judy A Davis
PO Box 292
Plymouth FL 32768
Information 407/ 298-0901
or 886-0260
Call Out 407/ 872-8099
or 263-2338

Florida Independent Dog
Handler Organization
Bill Frodl
PO Box 667
Astatula FL 34705
Information 904/ 343-0766
Call Out 800/ 241-4653

Florida Search Dog Assoc
Jennifer Tooker
Rte 2 Box 725-8
Micanopy FL 32667
Information 904/ 466-3090
Call Out 904/ 336-2413

Metro-Dade SAR Dogs
19570 Holiday Rd
Miami FL 33157
Information 305/ 255-0998
Call Out 305/ 596-8571

NW Florida SAR Squad
Nancy Jones
PO Box 257
Alford FL 32420
Info. & Call Out 904/ 579-4132
or 482-9669

South West Florida K-9 SAR
Charlene Schroder
19600 Pine Echo Rd
North Ft Meyers FL 33917
Information 813/ 543-2290

Special Response Team-A,
Florida Wing CAP
Lt Col E Wolff
PO Box 10581
Pompano Beach FL 33061
Information 305/ 943-0116
Call Out 800/ 255-1749

GEORGIA

Georgia K-9 Rescue Assoc
Sandra Crain
PO Box 12
Cusseta GA 31805
Information 404/ 989-3464
or 989-3648
Call Out 404/ 571-4939

Hamilton County STARS
Jim Poplin
114 Valley Breeze Trail
Roseville GA 30741
Information 404/ 861-1730
Call Out 615/ 757-2905

SAR Dogs of Gerogia
[SARDOG]
Allen or Karen Padgett
PO Box 662
Lafayette GA 30728
Information 706/ 638-4144
Call Out 706/ 865-3855

IDAHO

Intermountain SAR Dogs
Bob Langendoen
PO Box 1143
Ketchum ID 83340
Information 208/ 726-1842
Call Out 208/ 788-5555

Mountain West Rescue Dogs
Michael Anderson
509 Spokane St
Coeur d'Alene ID 83814
Information 208/ 664-5691
or 773-9437
Call Out 208/ 664-1511

ILLINOIS

Forest Preserve,
Du Page County Dog Unit
PO Box 2339
Glen Ellyn IL 60138
Information 708/ 920-1664
Call Out 708/ 790-4900 x 201

Hamilton County SAR
McLeansboro Fire Dept
209 E Brdway
McLeansboro IL 62859
Information 618/ 643-3829
Call Out 618/ 643-2233

Illini SAR Service
Mike Wiedel
24 W 640 Ohio St
Naperville IL 60540
Information 708/ 357-1271
Call Out 708/ 640-0102

Illinois/Wisconsin SAR Dogs
Patti Gibson
446 Porter Ave
Crystal Lake IL 60014
Information 815/ 459-6523
or 459-6442
Call Out 815/ 338-2143

RESAR
Bill Renaker
Box 425
Ingleside IL 60041
Information 708/ 587-2561
Call Out 708/ 587-3100

Springfield SAR K-9
Kay Watt
222 E Hazel Dell Ln

Springfield IL 62707
Information 529/ 7349

INDIANA

Indiana K-9 SAR
Don Rabe
94 Ashbourne
Noblesville IN 46060

SMART
Jeff Howell
PO Box 788
New Albany IN 47151
Information 812/ 945-4676
Call Out 812/ 948-5400

KANSAS

Black Paws Search & Rescue Dogs
Nicolette Dobson
515 E 10th St
Pittsburg KS 66762
Information 316/ 232-7010
Call Out 316/ 231-5377 pager

Lenexa Canine Unit
Pat Hinkle
12500 W 87th St
Lenexa KS 66205
Information & Call Out 913/ 888-4110

KENTUCKY

Jefferson Co EMS K-9 Unit
Jefferson Co EMS
7201 Outer Loop
Louisville KY 40228
Information 502/ 239-7110
Call Out 502/ 625-3636

Kentucky Search Dog Assoc
Patty Petzinger
R#4 Box 153
Owenton KY 40359
Information 502/ 484-3755
or 484-3417
Call Out 800/ 255-2587

LOUISIANA

LASAR-SAR Dogs
Dee Wild
PO Box 2477
Slidell LA 70459
Information 504/ 641-9769
Call Out 504/ 892-8181

MAINE

Maine SAR Dogs
Jennifer Applegate
80 Ledgelawn Ave
Bar Harbor ME 04609
Information 207/ 288-3882
Call Out 207/ 941-4440

Maine State Prison
Bloodhound Search Unit
Sgt John A Struk
Box A
Thomaston MA 04861
Information & Call Out 207/ 354-2535

Search Dogs Northeast
Perry Hopkins
PO Box 438
Alfred ME 04002
Information 207/ 324-3221
Call Out 800/ 585-6121

MARYLAND

Baltimore County Fire Dept
SAR Dog Unit
Lt Daniel Kluge
700 East Joppa Rd
Towson MD 21204
Information 301/ 378-4522 or 887-8100
Call Out 301/ 887-4592 or 887-2769

Mid-Atlantic DOGS Inc
Marian Hardy
4 Orchard Way North
Rockville MD 20854
Information 301/ 762-7217
Call Out 301/ 217-4644

SAR Dogs of Maryland
[ARDA-MD]

Bob Snyder
PO Box 545
White Plains MD 20695
Information 301/ 843-1609
Call Out 301/ 705-3546 pager

Southern Maryland SAR Dogs
Scott Earhart
365 Jones Wharf Rd
Hollywood MD 20636
Information 301/ 373-8259
Call Out 301/ 475-8016

MASSACHUSETTS

MASS Air Scenting K-9s
559 Peter Shan Rd
Athol MA 01331-9401
Information 508/ 249-6143
Call Out 508/ 355-4991

Martha's Vineyard K-9 Unit, Inc
Gina Hodges
PO Box 2277
17 Oklahoma Ave
Vineyard Haven MA 02568
Info. & Call Out 609/ 723-2760 or 508/ 693-7299

Mass Bay SAR Dogs
Donna Johnson
236 High St
Ipswich MA 01938
Information 508/ 356-7222

MICHIGAN

DOGS-North
Sally Santeford
RT 1 Box 332
Houghton MI 49931
Information 906/ 482-5135
Call Out 906/ 482-4411

Mid-Michigan Canine SAR Team
Mark Michalek
11512 Hazel Ave
Grand Blanc MI 48439
Information 313/ 695-2268
Call Out 313/ 257-3423

MINNESOTA

Arrowhead Search Dogs
Bill Mitchell
PO Box 468
Tower MN 55790
Information 218/ 365-2111
Call Out 218/ 741-7408

Minnesota SAR Dog Assoc
Kathy Newman
7335-223rd Ave NW
Elk River MN 55330
Information 612/ 441-3734
Call Out 612/ 427-1212

Northstar SAR Dog Assoc
Hans Erdman
PO Box 29134
Minneapolis MN 55429
Information 612/ 566-6236
Call Out 218/ 749-6010

Search Dogs Inc
Mary Jane Dyer
3310 Wren Ln
Eagan MN 55121
Information 612/ 452-4209

Southern Minnesota Canine SAR
Kathy Schroeder
28 7th St NE
Rochester MN 55904
Information 507/ 533-8015

MISSISSIPPI

DeSoto Co. Emergency
Management K-9
T H Walker
247 Losher
Hernando MS 38632
Information 601/ 429-1359
Call Out 601/ 429-1350

Gulf Coast SAR
Carlos Redmon
12397 N Oaklawn Ln
Biloxi MS 39532

Information 601/ 392-5419
Call Out 601/ 435-6150

MISSOURI

Black Paws Search, Rescue
& Avalanche Dogs
Richardson
16740 John's Cabin Rd
Glencoe MO 63038
Information 314/ 458-3248
Call Out 314/ 434-5500

Mid-America Rescue Dog Assoc
Karen Brown
HCR 77 Box 17-1
Sunrise Beach MO 65079
Information & Call Out 314/ 374-6388

Missouri SAR K-9
Irene Korotev
8307 Winchester
Kansas City MO 64138
Information 816/ 356-9097
Call Out 814/ 524-4300

Odessa VFD Bloodhounds
Orville Day
809 W Pleasant
Odessa MO 64076
Information 816/ 633-5396

Rainbow Mission SAR
Joyce Tolle
5865 Highway V
St Charles MO 63301
Information 314/ 258-3077
Call Out 314/ 949-3023

MONTANA

Absaroka Search Dogs
Vikki Fenton Bowman
2312 Pine St
Billings MT 59101
Information 406/ 245-7335
Call Out 406/ 322-5326

Black Paws SAR
Susie Foley

PO Box 684
Bigfork MT 59911
Information 406/ 837-5547
Call Out 406/ 883-4321

Lewis & Clark SAR Assoc
Ralph DeCunzo
PO Box 473
Helena MT 59624
Information 406/ 933-5962
Call Out 406/ 442-7880

Montana PAWS K-9 SAR
Kim Gilmore
PO Box 2081
Whitefish MT 59937-2081
Information 406/ 771-0139
Call Out 406/ 721-4516

Rivalli County SAR
Mary Jo Holmgren
PO Box 456
Stevensville MT 59870
Information 406/ 363-6312
Call Out 406/ 363-3033

Search Dogs North
Debbie Tirmenstein
PO Box 5254
Missoula MT 59806
Information 406/ 721-7256
Call Out 406/ 523-6044

NEW HAMPSHIRE

Granite State Search Dogs
Lisa Walpole
PO Box 126
Windham NH 03087
Information 603/ 434-3210

Granite State Search Dogs
Bill Peterson
PO Box 126
Windham NH 03087
Information 603/ 434-3210
Call Out 603/ 564-4521

New England K-9 SAR
Jo Ann Clark
RR 3 Box 38
St Johnsbury VT 05819
Information 802/ 748-6546
Call Out 603/ 352-3210

Strafford County Sheriff's
Bloodhound Unit
Penny Schroeder
RD 2 Box 726
Center Barnstead NH 03225
Information 603/ 269-5461
Call Out 603/ 742-4960

NEW JERSEY

Cape May County Sheriff's Dept
Col William Donohue
Crest Haven Complex
Cape May Court House NJ 08210
Information 609/ 889-6560
Call Out 609/ 465-1237

Palisades SAR Dog Assoc
April Pampalone
291 Main St
Milburn NJ 07041
Information 201/ 376-7377
Call Out 201/ 993-7868 pager

Ramapo Rescue Dog Assoc
Penny Sullivan
Goose Pond Mountain State Park
PO Box 151
Chester NY 10918
Information 914/ 469-4173
Call Out 201/ 664-1111

Watchung Mountain K-9 SAR
Barry Orange
1091 Raritan Rd
Clark NJ 07066
Information 908/ 381-3182
Call Out 800/ 631-3444

West Jersey Canine SAR
PO Box 205
Pittstown NJ 08867

Information 908/ 236-2387
Call Out 908/ 788-1202

NEW MEXICO

Albuquerque Rescue Dog Assoc
Diana Pappan
1037 Stuart Rd NW
Albuquerque NM 87114

Cibola SAR
Bruce Berry
10725 Edith NE
Albuquerque NM 87113
Information 505/ 897-3652
Call Out 505/ 827-9226

Four Corners SAR
Ed Hoog
PO Box 1921
Farmington NM 87499
Information 505/ 632-8525

Mountain Canine Corps
Terry DuBois
2896-B Walnut
Los Alamos NM 87544
Information 505/ 662-9605
Call Out 505/ 827-9226

New Mexico Bloodhound Assoc
Bill Bailey
801 Quincy NE
Albuquerque NM 87110
Information 505/ 255-7745
Call Out 505/ 827-9226

New Mexico Rescue Dogs
Bob Foster
80 Raven Rd
Tijeras NM 87059
Information 505/ 281-3975
Call Out 505/ 827-9226

NEW YORK

American/Adirondack Rescue Dog Assoc
Marilyn Green
5028 Juniper Ln

Schenectady NY 12303
Information 518/ 356-2431
Call Out 518/ 462-6964
 Amigo K-9 SAR Team
Ed Rivera
RD 2 Box 77B Janke Rd
Delhi NY 13753
Information & Call Out 607/ 746-3647

Heritage K-9 Search &
Rescue Tracking Service
Pat & Tim Karas
216 Rumsey Hill
Van Etten NY 14889
Information 607/ 589-4246
Call Out 607/ 776-2165

Massassauga SAR Team
Larry Fleming
PO Box 518
Fairport NY 14450
Information 716/ 461-9470
Call Out 716/ 343-2200

Rensselaer County SAR Team
David Onderdonk
Onderdonk Ave
Rensselaer NY 12144
Information 518/ 477-9267
Call Out 518/ 479-1212

Wilderness SAR Team
Rick Reardon
202 Lynhurst Ave
N Syracuse NY 13212
Information 315/ 458-7509
Call Out 315/ 425-3333

Yates County Sheriff's Dept
Sheriff Jan Scofield
106 Seneca St Box 116
Dundee NY 14527
Information 607/ 243-7501
Call Out 315/ 536-4438

NORTH CAROLINA

Blue Ridge SAR Dogs
Brenda Davis

225 Stewart Rd
Waynesville NC 28786

Burke County Rescue Squad
Michael Metcalf
PO Box 371
Morganton NC 28655
Information 704/ 584-1387
Call Out 704/ 437-1911

North Carolina SAR Assoc
Denver Holder
Clyde NC 28721
Information 704/ 648-3851
Call Out 704/ 255-5631

Piney Grove Search Team
Capt Ken Young
1109 Piney Grove Rd
Kernersville NC 27284
Information 919/ 996-4244
Call Out 919/ 727-2222

Raleigh Fire Dept
Ray Bradford
1305 Broken Br Ct
Raleigh NC 27610
Information 919/ 231-1938
Call Out 919/ 831-6331

Safeway SAR
Wayne May
PO Box 691
Coats NC 27521
Information 919/ 897-3197

Search Dog Services Inc
Mac McClure
177 Chiles Ave
Asheville NC 28803
Information & Call Out 704/ 252-3291

NORTH DAKOTA

Black Paws Search, Rescue
& Avalanche Dogs
David Oehike
PO Box 823
Devils Lake ND 58301

Information 701/ 662-8587
Call Out 701/ 662-5323

OHIO

Athens Search, Track & Rescue
Jon Tobin
74 E State St
Athens OH 45701
Information 614/ 592-4630
Call Out 594-2261

Marblehead K-9 Unit, Inc
Jim Zarifis
PO Box 3
Marblehead OH 43440
Information & Call Out 419/ 798-4942

Ohio K-9 Search Team, Inc
Donna Stusek
PO Box 02200
Columbus OH 43202
Information 614/ 569-4855

Stonehill Mantrailers
Donna Stone
2146 Eden Rd
Hamersville OH 45130
Information 513/ 379-9301
Call Out 513/ 249-3572 pager

Tri-Star SAR
Donna Stone
2146 Eden Rd
Hammerville OH 45130
Information 513/ 379-9301

OKLAHOMA

Oklahoma K-9 SAR
Mike Nozer
4808 S Elwood
Tulsa OK 74101
Information 918/ 445-2291
Call Out 918/ 596-5601

Rescue Dogs of NE Oklahoma
Sharon Kyle
8544 E 11th

Tulsa OK 74112
SAR Dogs of Oklahoma
Tracy Fox
4119 E Zion St
Tulsa OK 74115
Information 918/ 836-7139
Call Out 918/ 596-5657

Western Ozark Bloodhound Team
Elsa Gann
RT 2 Box 162
Collinsville OK 74021

OREGON

Independent SAR Dog Assoc
David Graf
PO Box 1646
Tualatin OR 97062

Mountain Wilderness Search Dogs
Harry Oakes
PO Box 30364
Portland OR 97230
Information 503/ 650-1904
Call Out 503/ 650-1904

Search One SAR Dogs
Bill Ridings
7981 SW Nyberg Rd
Tualatin OR 97062
Info & Call Out 503/ 297-5540
or 231-2056

PENNSYLVANIA

Black Paws Search, Rescue
& Avalanche Dogs
Curtis Settle
RR2 Box 324
Portage PA 15946
Information 814/ 696-4112

Dept of Environmental Resources
SAR Unit
Ken Boyles
1599 Doubling Gap Rd
Newville PA 17241
Information 717/ 776-7949

Call Out 717/ 776-5272 pager

Dog Team 200
Joe Thrash
RD 1 Box 75
Fridens PA 15541
Information 814/ 445-4762
Call Out 814/ 445-4133

Friendship Fire Co K-9
SAR Unit
Susan & Larry Bulanda
106 Halteman Rd
Pottstown PA 19464
Information 610/ 323-8022
Call Out 610/ 469-7617 pager

Greensburg Fire Dept
Bloodhound Team
Edward Hutchinson
318 Alexander Ave
Greensburg PA 15601
Information 412/ 834-7365
Call Out 412/ 834-7007

Northeast SAR
Bruce Barton
PO Box 162
Stroudsburg PA 18360
Information 717/ 424-1883
Call Out 800/ 426-3647

Red Rose K-9 SAR Team
Allen & Patti Means
431 Weaver Rd
Strasburg PA 17579
Information 717/ 293-4432
Call Out 717/ 687-8873

Rescue 40
Patty Depp
21 Norwich Ave
Pittsburg PA 15229
Information 412/ 931-0590
Call Out 216/ 775-0880

STRIKE K-9
Carol Prosseda
PO Box 61

West Milton PA 17886
Information 717/ 742-8555
Call Out 717/ 742-8771

Thornhurst Volunteer Fire Rescue
Jim Howley
HC Box 119
Thornhurst PA 18424
Information 717/ 842-9412
Call Out 717/ 342-9111

Tri-County SAR K-9 Unit
Linda Good
RR# 1 Box 488
Mill Hall PA 17751
Information 717/ 726-4714

White Deer SAR
John & Kim Carr
PO Box 93
New Columbia PA 17856
Information 717/ 568-0567
Call Out 717/ 568-0567

SOUTH CAROLINA

Cross Creek Training Academy
Dondi Hydrick
PO Box 7368
North Augusta SC 29841
Information 803/ 279-8716

SOUTH DAKOTA

Dakota SAR Dog Team
Dick Ness
204 S 4th Ave
Brandon SD 57005-1248
Information605/ 745-4600
Call Out 605/ 339-2335

Nancy Dineen
110 E Van Duren
Rapid City SD 57701
Information 605/ 348-8515

TENNESSEE

Morristown Emergency

& Rescue Squad
Jackye Byrd
420 N Jackson St
Morristown TN 37814
Information 615/ 581-4469
Call Out 615/ 586-1314

TEXAS

CESAR
Tim Samsill
4704 Susan Lee Ln
North Richland Hills TX 76180
Information 817/ 577-2055
Call Out 817/ 581-4313

Law Enforcement Training Specialist
Sgt Billy Smith
1803 FM 656 Box C-1
Rosharon TX 77583
Information 713/ 595-3276
Call Out 713/ 595-2590

North Texas Volunteer Mantrailers
Teri Anglim
3805 Misty Meadow
Ft Worth TX 76133
Information 817/ 294-8740
Call Out 817/ 469-3976

San Angelo Rescue Dogs
Eddie Howard
3818 Deerfield Rd
San Angelo TX 76904
Information 915/ 944-1288
or 800/ 627-8916
Call Out 915/ 657-4356
or 915/ 658-8111

Search One
David Brownell
555 Northridge Dr
Allen TX 75002

South Texas SAR K-9 Unit
Juan Gonzaba
2105 Lemon Tree Court
Edinburg TX 78539
Information 512/ 381-8080

Call Out 512/ 383-8114
Starr County Sheriff K-9 Unit
Eugenio Falcon Jr
Starr County Courthouse
Rio Grande City TX 78582
Call Out 512/ 487-5571

Texas EMT Dog Unit/TEXSSAR
Ron Perry
3010 Sierra Dr
San Angelo TX 76904
Information 915/ 944-2139
Call Out 915/ 657-4356

Texas Search Dogs Assoc
Bobby Farquhar
2617 Oakwood Terr
Ft. Worth TX 76117
Information 817/ 838-3198
Call Out 817/ 432-5423

UTAH

American Search Dogs
Bob Ellis
4939 Ben Lomond Ave
South Ogden UT 84403
Information 801/ 476-9544
Call Out 801/ 451-3555

Rocky Mountain Rescue Dogs
Barbara Altum
3353 S Main St #122
Salt Lake City UT 84115-4457
Information 801/ 742-2469
Call Out 801/ 535-5855

VERMONT

Vermont SAR Dog Service
Mary Anne Gummere
PO Box 4
Barton VT 05822
Information 802/ 525-6253
Call Out 802/ 748-8141 x 436

VIRGINIA

Blue & Gray SAR Dogs

Vicki Michael
RT 3 Box 272-1
Dayton VA 22821
Information 703/ 869-1520
Call Out 703/ 879-9684 pager

Colonial Heights SAR Unit
Willie Jenkins
903 Kensington Ave
Colonial Heights VA 23834
Information 804/ 520-2056
Call Out 804/ 520-9300

DOGS East
Ed Johnson
136 Indiantown Rd
King George VA 22485
Information 703/ 775-9568
Call Out 800/ 468-8892

K-9 Alert SAR Dogs
Winnie Pennington
2732 Grantwood Rd
Richmond VA 23225
Information 804/ 320-8052
Call Out 804/ 674-2400

Search Services America, Inc
Cody Perry
PO Box 159
Goldvein VA 22720
Information 703/ 752-2394
Call Out 804/ 674-2400

Sussex County Sheriff's Dept Office
Philip Andrews
RT 2 Box 172A
Disputanta VA 23842
Information 804/ 834-3528
Call Out 804/ 246-5361

Tazewell County Sheriff's Dept
Clarence Tatum
RT 2 Box 21A
Cedar Bluff VA 24609
Information 703/ 964-4859

Tidewater Trail SAR Team
Ginger Branyon

111 Creek Circle
Seaford VA 23696
Information 804/ 898-7118
Call Out 800/ 468-8892

Virginia Bloodhound SAR Assoc
PO Box 229
Leesburg VA 22075

Virginia SAR Dogs
Alice Stanley
RT 1 Box 1508
Woodford VA 22580
Information 703/ 582-5708
Call Out 703/ 659-4133

WASHINGTON

Black Paws Search, Rescue
& Avalanche Dogs
Cynthia Baker
17907 26th St Ct
E Summer WA 98390
Information 206/ 393-0900
Call Out 206/ 862-1825

Cascade Dogs
Rich & Kathy Fifer
129 Wiatrak Rd
Morton WA 98356
Information 206/ 496-5184
Call Out 800/ 562-5620

Clark County SAR
10810 NE 67th St
Vancouver WA 98662
Information & Call Out 206/ 892-1386

Dog Alert Rescue Team
Lori Matlock
327 S Main
Colville WA 99114
Information 509/ 684-4481
Call Out 509/ 684-2555

German Shepherd Search Dogs
of Washington State
Bruce Cheshier
3202 Burnett Ave N

Renton WA 98056
Information 206/ 228-3278
Call Out 206/ 432-5855

Justice Search Dogs
Jan Tweedie
12309 SE 164th
Renton WA 98058
Information 206/ 255-6852
Call Out 206/ 969-2584

Mantrackers and Search Dogs
Alice Webber
10810 NE 67th St
Vancouver WA 98662
Information 206/ 892-5842
Call Out 509/ 427-8076

Northwest Bloodhounds SAR
Jan Tweedie
12309 SE 164th
Renton WA 98058
Information 206/ 255-6852

Pacific Rim Disaster Team
Marcia Koening
1155 North 130th St #420
Seattle WA 98133
Information 206/ 823-6030
Call Out 206/ 367-7712 pager or
206/ 995-2202

Sandpoint Cadet Squadron
Bloodhound Team
Tim Vik
7309 Sandpoint Wy NE 838
Seattle WA 98115
Information 206/ 526-0332

West Coast Search Dogs
Terre Reeson
512 W 5th St
Hoquiam WA 98550
Information 206/ 533-2790
Call Out 206/ 249-3911

WEST VIRGINIA

West Virginia K-9 SAR

Jack Coon
2489 Dudden Fork
Kenna WV 25248
Information 304/ 988-9775
Call Out 304/ 348-5380

WISCONSIN

Badgerland Search Dogs
Robert Streich
957 Lawrence St
Madison WI 53715

Dane County Sheriff K-9 Unit
Carl Koehler
626 Eagle Watch Dr
De Forest WI 53532-3044
Information 608/ 249-0208
Call Out 608/ 266-4948

Headwaters SAR Dog Assoc
Jill Lemke
441 Mian St
Sayner WI 54560
Information 715/ 545-3837
Call Out 715/ 479-4441

Minocqua Police Dept
Bloodhound Unit
Gerry Frigge
PO Box 636
Woodruff WI 54568
Information 715/ 356-9318
Call Out 715/ 356-3234

RescuMed Dog Assoc
Lori Wick
1304 W Terminal Rd
Grafton WI 53024
Information 414/ 375-0456
Call Out 414/ 425-2944

Wilderness SAR
Lois Kuntz
PO Box 9
Phillips WI 54555

Info & Call Out 715/ 682-5592
Woodruff Police Dept
Bloodhound Unit
Gerry Figge
PO Box 636
Woodruff WI 54568
Information 715/ 356-9318

WYOMING

Park County Sheriff
Linda Waggoner
1131 11th St
Cody WY 82414
Info & Call Out 307/ 587-5524

Star Valley SAR
Dep Timothy Malik
Lincoln Co SO
Afton WY 83110

INDEX